MW01105904

OUTDOOR FURNITURE

FOR THE **Weekend Woodworker**

RODALE'S STEP-BY-STEP GUIDE TO

OUTDOOR FURNITURE

FOR THE Weekend Woodworker

Stylish Projects for the Yard and Deck

BILL HYLTON with **Fred Matlack and Phil Gehret**
Illustrations by Frank Rohrbach
Photos by Mitch Mandel

Rodale Press, Inc.
Emmaus, Pennsylvania

© 1995 by Rodale Press, Inc.
Illustrations © 1995 by Frank Rohrbach

All rights reserved. No part of this publication may be reproduced or transmitted in any form or by any means, electronic or mechanical, including photocopy, recording, or any other information storage and retrieval system, without the written permission of the publisher.

The authors and editors who compiled this book have tried to make all of the contents as accurate and as correct as possible. Plans, illustrations, photographs, and text have all been carefully checked and cross-checked. However, due to the variability of local conditions, construction materials, personal skill, and so on, neither the authors nor Rodale Press assumes any responsibility for any injuries suffered or for damages or other losses incurred that result from the material presented herein. All instructions and plans should be carefully studied and clearly understood before beginning construction.

Printed in the United States of America on acid-free ∞, recycled ♲ paper, containing 20 percent post-consumer waste

This book is reprinted in part from *Outdoor Furniture,* previously published by Rodale Press, Inc.

Library of Congress Cataloging-in-Publication Data

Hylton, Bill.
  [Outdoor furniture. Selections]
  Outdoor furniture for the weekend woodworker : stylish projects for the yard and deck / Bill Hylton with Fred Matlack and Phil Gehret ; illustrations by Frank Rohrbach.
      p.   cm.
  Fifteen woodworking projects taken from Outdoor furniture (Rodale Press, 1992)
  ISBN 0–87596–727–2 (pbk. : alk. paper)
  1. Outdoor furniture. 2. Furniture making.
I. Matlack, Fred. II. Gehret, Phil. III. Title
TT197.5.09H962 1995b
684.1'8—dc20   95–8984

Distributed in the book trade by St. Martin's Press

2 4 6 8 10 9 7 5 3 1   paperback

OUTDOOR FURNITURE FOR THE WEEKEND WOODWORKER

EDITORIAL STAFF
Cover Designer: Frank M. Milloni
Photographer: Mitch Mandel
Interior Book Designer: Jerry O'Brien
Illustrator: Frank Rohrbach
Designers of projects: Fred Matlack and Phil Gehret
Copy Editor: Sarah Dunn
Production Coordinator: Patrick T. Smith

RODALE BOOKS
Editorial Director, Home and Garden:
    Margaret Lydic Balitas
Managing Editor, Woodworking and DIY Books:
    Kevin Ireland
Art Director, Home and Garden:
    Michael Mandarano
Associate Art Director, Home and Garden:
    Mary Ellen Fanelli
Copy Director, Home and Garden:
    Dolores Plikaitis
Office Manager, Home and Garden:
    Karen Earl-Braymer
Editor-in-Chief: William Gottlieb

On the front cover: A view of the Terrace Table and Chairs, found on page 14. *On the back cover:* The Vineyard Ensemble, found on page 87, and the Oak Porch Swing, found on page 112.

If you have any questions or comments concerning this book, please write to:
    Rodale Press, Inc.
    Book Readers' Service
    33 East Minor Street
    Emmaus, PA 18098

—— OUR MISSION ——
We publish books that empower people's lives.

R O D A L E   BOOKS

CONTENTS

INTRODUCTION

If you are looking for some out-of-the-ordinary outdoor furniture you can build yourself, look no further. This collection of projects is it.

Prove it to yourself. Go ahead: Flip through the pages, if you haven't already. Check out what the book has to show you. You'll see these are not 2 × 4 picnic table projects. This is a collection for real woodworkers, those who have advanced beyond nailed butt joints. If you've got a table saw or radial arm saw, if you've got a router, you can build these tables and chairs and loungers.

When we designed this small collection, we wanted classy, comfortable, practical, *durable* outdoor stuff. What we came up with are show pieces that aren't likely to turn up at the local K-Wal or Lumber Emporium. The only way your neighbor will get furniture like this is if he makes it for himself.

In creating the plans in this book, our goal was to present each project in thorough, lucid detail. Assuming that you already have a book or two on woodworking, we included nothing in *OUTDOOR FURNITURE FOR THE WEEKEND WOODWORKER* but projects. There's no chapter on techniques, no appendix with a rundown on tools or joints or glues.

It's just projects.

And what a showcase of outdoor furniture. We've got an easy-to-make mahogany chair and settee for sitting on the deck or patio, elegant oak chairs and a table for terrace dining, and a cushioned cedar chair and settee—with ottoman—for when you need to relax in the cool shade with your feet up. Want to stretch out in the sun? There's a mahogany designer chaise lounge with a cushy

pad. Want to swing on the porch? How about our oak porch swing. There are other projects as well.

The project presentations are shaped to serve a diversity of needs. Skim through the pages again: Highlighted tips and how-to photos present time-saving shortcuts and proven techniques you can use in *any project*. Page more slowly: Photos show what the finished projects look like in typical backyard settings. "Builder's Notes" discuss the salient aspects of every project. Where a specific tool or glue or finish is pertinent to the project, detailed information about it is presented in the notes. Tool and shopping lists let you know what tools are necessary and how much wood is required; you won't get started on a project that you can't complete.

Once you do start, the information you need is all there. Dimensioned drawings, gridded patterns, isolated details—we've got scores of revealing and helpful two-color drawings. Clarifying important woodworking operations and assembly procedures are dozens of how-to photos. Step-by-step directions list the work sequence and describe *how* to do the tasks necessary to build each project. All of these features support you weekend woodworkers as you build a project.

As for those of you who are veteran woodworkers, who don't need—or want—all the guidance, you can simply peruse the Cutting List and dimensioned illustrations and set to work. If a technique is unfamiliar, the explanation is there.

And don't assume that there are no challenges in *OUTDOOR FURNITURE FOR THE WEEKEND WOODWORKER*. The Terrace Ensemble—table and four chairs with a 10-foot-diameter canvas-covered umbrella—is handsome and expensive-looking, with its mortise-and-tenon construction in solid oak. Too, there's the Vineyard Ensemble, that deep-cushioned chair with an ottoman and a flagstone-topped side table: It's a deceptively challenging project that demands you know how to use your band saw.

As you've doubtless noted, none of these projects is in redwood. One ensemble is made of cedar, and one is made of mahogany. You can substitute redwood for these projects. Or even pine. But several are built of oak. For these, stick with oak or some other strong hardwood.

Bill Hylton has been writing and editing Rodale Press books for more than 20 years. He created Rodale's first woodworking title, *Build It Better Yourself,* as well as its most recent backyard building title, *Projects for Outdoor Living*. **Fred Matlack** and **Phil Gehret** have been building projects for Rodale's magazines and books for 15 years. They've designed and constructed hundreds of projects, ranging from solar food driers to toys to antique reproductions. All the projects in *OUTDOOR FURNITURE FOR THE WEEKEND WOODWORKER* were designed and constructed by Fred 'n' Phil.

TRUNDLE CHAISE

A Web-Seated Armchair with Pull-Out Footrest

This nifty chair and footrest was inspired by a wicker chaise I saw in a catalog of high-tone garden furniture. We liked the form of the piece, but making a *wicker* project . . .? Fred Matlack, who runs Rodale's woodworking shop, worked the form in his mind and came up with this version.

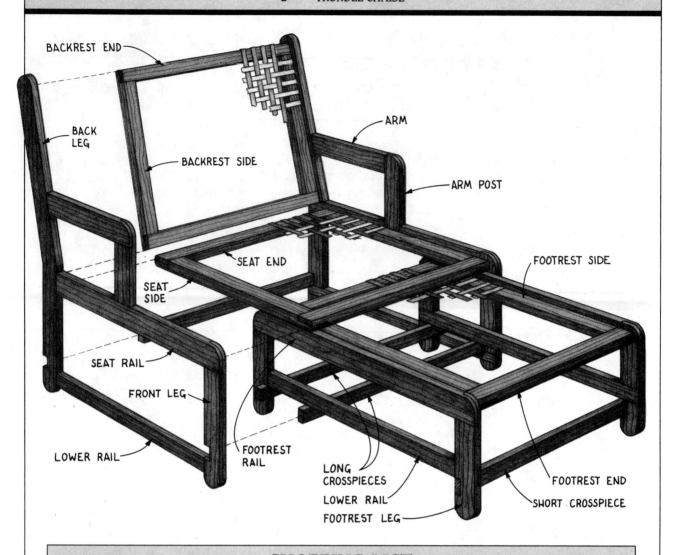

SHOPPING LIST

LUMBER
4½ bd. ft. 5/4 white oak
10½ bd. ft. 4/4 white oak

HARDWARE AND SUPPLIES
100 yd. (approx.) 1" wide cotton webbing
12 pcs. 16 ga. × ½" nails
44 pcs. #8 × 2" brass flathead screws

HARDWARE AND SUPPLIES—CONTINUED
16 pcs. #8 brass finish washers
Resorcinol glue

FINISH
Exterior-grade penetrating oil

The piece is a collection of half-lap frames. Three rectangular ones are for the woven seat and back and footrest. Four others are the side frames (two for the chair, two for the footrest). The seat and back are joined to the side frames with screws. We selected brass flathead screws with brass finish washers; these say, "Yeah, we're screws holding this together, but we're wearing our good duds."

Fred used oak for the frames, after trying pine. The pine simply didn't seem substantial enough to "take" the weaving. The weaving is inch-wide cotton webbing purchased at a local tent, canopy, and awning company. It really is black and white.

I like this chair a lot. It is surprisingly comfortable. The weaving is firm, and the back is fairly erect. With a couple of scatter pillows under the small of your back,

CUTTING LIST

PIECE	NUMBER	THICKNESS	WIDTH	LENGTH	MATERIAL
Web frames					
Seat/footrest sides	4	1⅛"	1½"	30"	5/4 oak
Backrest sides	2	1⅛"	1½"	22"	5/4 oak
Seat/backrest ends	4	1⅛"	1½"	24"	5/4 oak
Footrest ends	2	1⅛"	1½"	22"	5/4 oak
Side frames					
Back legs	2	¾"	5"	36"	4/4 oak
Seat rails	2	¾"	2½"	33½"	4/4 oak
Front legs	2	¾"	2½"	14"	4/4 oak
Arms	2	¾"	2½"	19½"	4/4 oak
Arm posts	2	¾"	2½"	11½"	4/4 oak
Lower rails	4	¾"	1½"	33"	4/4 oak
Footrest rails	2	¾"	2½"	33"	4/4 oak
Footrest legs	4	¾"	2½"	12"	4/4 oak
Long crosspieces	3	¾"	1½"	25⅝"	4/4 oak
Short crosspiece	1	¾"	1½"	23⅝"	4/4 oak

it's a great chair for reading, where you want to be sort of erect but not bolt upright. And the weaving does have give without being saggy and hammocky. Moreover, the proportions and dimensions of the chair are tailored to someone my size (a bulky 6 footer).

A feature of the piece that I like, and that prompted the name, is that the footrest is interconnected with the chair. You can slide it in under the chair to get it out of the way. But because they're interlinked, you can't pick up the chair without also picking up the footrest.

Builder's Notes

You face mostly modest challenges with this project. The frame is put together with half-laps, a relatively simple joint. The weaving requires little skill but a generous measure of patience. Expect to spend two or three hours weaving each of the three panels.

Materials. A prototype web frame made of pine didn't hold up quite as well to the stresses of all those taut webs as Fred Matlack had hoped. He switched to a strong, easily available (in our area, anyway) hardwood, white oak. In addition to greater strength than pine, the oak has greater decay resistance. But oak's sturdiness comes at the price of weight—and keep in mind that the footrest doesn't detach.

You could switch to some other hardwoods—the decay resistance of cherry, locust, and walnut compares favorably with that of the white oak. But these three woods are premium materials. Hardwoods like poplar and maple, plentiful in many parts of the country, are poor choices for outdoor projects because of the low decay resistance. (I suggest hardwoods because it doesn't seem that the traditional outdoor woods—redwood and cedar—would be any better under stress than pine.) A compromise would be to make the web frames from oak, and the side frames from another stock.

If you've never tackled a hardwood project, this is actually a good one to start with. The required pieces are relatively uniform in width; the joinery is basic. And the finished project is very practical.

As I've noted with other projects, hardwoods aren't stocked by every lumberyard or building center. Where they are, you'll find them in rough-sawn form. The thicknesses are standardized, but the widths and lengths of individual boards are random. You have to keep the "Cutting List" handy so you select boards that will economically yield all the parts you need. And unless you have a jointer and a thickness planer, you'll need to have the dealer dress the boards you buy.

It should take only a phone call or two to track down a source for the 1-inch-wide cotton webbing (sometimes called tape). In our area, it's available both from a canopy and awning business, and from fabric stores. If you want or need to order it through the mail, try Shaker Workshops, P.O. Box 1028, Concord, MA 01742, or Connecticut Cane and Reed Company, P.O. Box 1276, Manchester, CT 06040. We used white and black web-

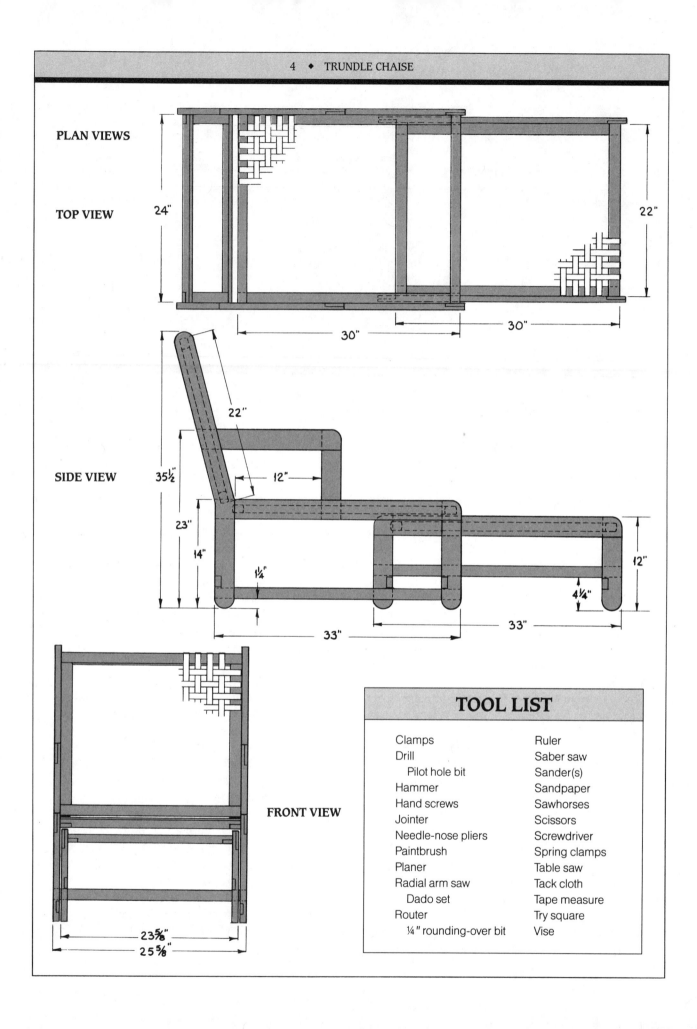

PLAN VIEWS

TOP VIEW

24"

22"

30"

30"

SIDE VIEW

22"

35½"

12"

23"

14"

1¼"

33"

33"

12"

4¼"

FRONT VIEW

23⅝"

25⅝"

TOOL LIST

Clamps	Ruler
Drill	Saber saw
Pilot hole bit	Sander(s)
Hammer	Sandpaper
Hand screws	Sawhorses
Jointer	Scissors
Needle-nose pliers	Screwdriver
Paintbrush	Spring clamps
Planer	Table saw
Radial arm saw	Tack cloth
Dado set	Tape measure
Router	Try square
¼" rounding-over bit	Vise

bing for a starkly geometric effect, but many colors are available. Use your imagination.

Tools and techniques. The joinery is fairly simple, and thus the required tools are typical of the hobby woodworker's shop. To dress the wood, you should have a jointer and a table saw, at a minimum. But since you can have the wood planed when you buy it—for an additional charge, of course—you don't absolutely need the jointer.

Half-lap joints are little trouble if made with a radial arm saw and a dado blade. The blade does the work with repeated passes over the lap, in full view. A router will serve well enough; so will a table saw and a dado blade, although you won't be able to monitor the blade's progress.

What shaping of parts is necessary can be accomplished satisfactorily with a saber saw, though a band saw would make quicker work of it.

No special tools are needed to do the webbing.

Two slightly different routes present themselves to the builder of this project. To build the chaise along the first route, you would cut the parts, build the frames, apply a finish to the entire project, do the weaving, and finally, assemble the piece. By the other, you would build and finish the web frames, then start the weaving. While the weaving is progressing, you take woodworking breaks and build and finish the side frames. At about the time the weaving is completed, the side frames are too, and the piece can be assembled.

In the following step-by-step directions, we take the latter approach. At about three hours per panel, the weaving is time-consuming. And unless you have an unusually large collection of clamps, you will need to glue up the frames one or two at a time.

Finish. The finish used on this chaise is CWF, a favorite of the Rodale woodworkers. A penetrating oil, it goes on quickly in two coats applied about a half-hour apart. You don't have to sand the project between coats. Since both coats go on in the same work session, you only have to clean up once. So using CWF—or any other penetrating oil graded for outdoor use—minimizes a task that, to a lot of us woodworkers, is really a chore.

Lest you forget, you do have to apply the finish to the web frames before you weave them. If penetrating oil is what you use, allow them to dry thoroughly before beginning the weaving.

1. Prepare the stock. Hardwood, as you know, generally is stocked in a rough-sawn state. To prepare it for use, you need to joint and plane it to reduce it to working thicknesses and to smooth the faces and edges.

Generally, this routine is followed:

• Crosscut the boards to rough working lengths first. That is, assuming the stock is close to the desired width, you measure off each part, allowing an extra inch or so, and crosscut it.

• Smooth one face on the jointer, making as many passes as necessary to really smooth it and remove all the saw marks.

• Joint one edge. Hold the jointed face against the jointer fence as you joint the edge; this will ensure that the edge is square to that face.

• Turn to the planer. Run the board through the planer as many times as is required to reduce the board to the desired thickness, resetting the cutters after each pass. (When planing a lot of parts, the usual practice is to set the planer, run all of them through, reset the planer and run them all through again, and so forth. That way, all the boards will end up at the same thickness.)

• Rip the boards to within 1/16 inch of the final width, then trim away that last 1/16 inch—and at the same time smooth away the saw marks—on the jointer.

The result is a board whose surfaces are flat and at right angles to their neighbors, and whose faces are parallel to each other.

There are some alternatives, although the results won't always be ideal.

If you lack a planer, you can often get away with jointing a face and an edge, then resawing the rough face on the table saw and cleaning up the cut on the jointer. The faces will be flat, but they may not be perfectly parallel.

If you lack a jointer, you can smooth both faces in a planer, and hand plane the edges. Here, one potential shortcoming is that the edges will be out of square with the faces. Another is that the faces won't be absolutely flat (the feed rollers of a big planer can exert enough pressure on a cupped board to flatten it; when the pressure is off the board, it recups.)

The obvious solution—and it can be a time-saver as well, if you are pressed for shop time—is to buy from a lumberyard or dealer that can surface the boards to your specifications.

2. Cut and assemble the parts for the web frames. Each web frame is simple: four lengths of wood joined together into a rectangle with half-lap joints. Each frame is a different size, but the frame members are all the same girth, so the laps to be cut are all the same. For each frame, cut two sides and two ends to the sizes specified by the "Cutting List." Mark an identification on each piece, so you know which frame it is for.

Cut the laps next. Possibly the best tool for cutting laps is the radial arm saw equipped with a dado cutter. Clamp a block to the backstop to govern the length of the lap. When the workpiece is butted to the block, the cutter will make the shoulder cut. Pull the workpiece back from the block and make another pass or two with the cutter to complete the lap. The workpiece is always sta-

tionary when it's being cut, the cut is not concealed from your view (as it is on the table saw), and the dado cutter hogs away a major amount of the waste with each pass.

With the laps completed, glue the frames together. Use resorcinol glue and pinch each joint with a hand screw, speed clamp, spring clamp, or the like until the glue sets. As you apply the clamps, be sure the frame is square and flat.

After the glue has set and the clamps are off, sand the frames carefully. Radius the edges, inside and out, top and bottom, with a router and a ¼-inch rounding-over bit. Dust the frames with a tack cloth, then apply two coats of an exterior-grade penetrating oil, with the second coat going on within a half hour of the first, when it is still wet.

WEB FRAME JOINERY

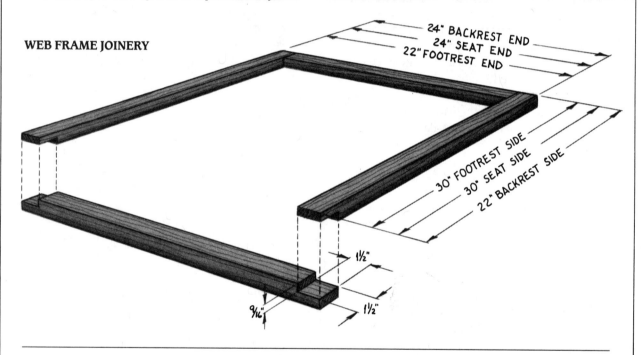

3. String the warp on a web frame. You'll weave the three web frames one at a time. And while work on the weaving is progressing, you can move ahead on building and finishing the side frames. The weaving is done in two steps: stringing the warp, and weaving. Stringing the warp is easy. The actual weaving takes far more time.

The warp is the aggregation of webs through which the weaver is interlaced. String the warp webbing on the frame from end to end. Nail the starting end to the frame near a corner. You could simply loop it around the outside of the frame, but there's a good possibility it will

simply slip off if the frame should get tipped the wrong way. Moreover, weaving on such a warp is somewhat more difficult. It's better to loop the webbing under and over the end frame members, as shown in *Stringing the Warp,* in a figure-eight course.

STRINGING THE WARP

Top: The starting end of the webbing is attached to the frame with a ½-inch nail. These nails are pretty small, so save your fingers and use needle-nose pliers to hold it for the first couple of hammer blows. Then wrap the webbing around itself and the frame member, covering the nail, before stretching it to the opposite end of the frame. Note that the attachment point is about ½ inch from the inside corner.

Center: String the warp in a figure-eight course; that is, over one frame member and under the opposite one. Leave the warp somewhat slack, and keep the loops a little more than the width of the tape apart. All of these things will help ease the job of weaving. Incidentally, note the size of the webbing roll.

Bottom: To tack down the end of the tape, crowd the second-to-last loop with the last. Wind the tape around the frame member and tack it down, just as you did the starting end. Then pull the last loop into its proper position, as shown, covering the nail and the end.

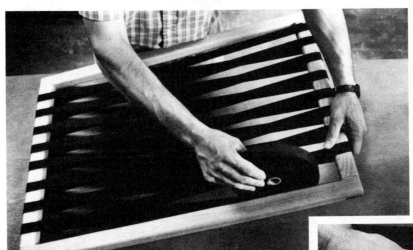

Before cutting the web and tacking the end, secure it with a spring clamp and adjust the spacing and tension of the webbing. Fred Matlack, who built and wove the chaise, provides two "don'ts."

• *Don't* make the warp too tight. As you weave, it tightens dramatically, and if you start with it too tight, you'll never be able to complete the weaving. Try to duplicate the tension shown in the photograph; the strands don't sag noticeably.

• *Don't* get the warp strands too close together. Weaving becomes extremely difficult. Each strand should be slightly more than the tape's width away from its neighbors.

When you are satisfied with your warp, cut off the webbing with enough margin to allow you to wrap it around the frame and nail it. Note that the last strand is pushed aside temporarily so that the nail can be driven. After the warp is secured, work the strand back in place to conceal the nailed end.

TIP

Since you don't want to be passing the entire roll of webbing through the warp, you need to cut a weaver. But you can't splice the webbing if you run short, so you need to estimate pretty accurately how long the weaver must be.

Do this: Nail the starting end in place and then simply wrap the correct number of courses around the frame, as shown. Don't bother interweaving the weave with the warp—this is just a trial run. When you've finished, add an extra margin for error, and cut. If you *do* end up short, there's a way to avoid having to cut another length of webbing and starting over. Back out the last course of weave, and reposition each previous course so that you can get by with one fewer.

4. **Weave the panel.** The weaver is very well named—it requires you to snake a strand into the warp. To make it easier to fish the weave through those tight places, use only as much webbing as you think the job will take, cutting that amount off the roll. Another way to speed the job along is to anchor the frame in a vise, so it is held upright at a comfortable working height, leaving both hands free.

Attach the weaver (which is often called the woof or the weft) as you did the warp. Nail the starting end of

Because the weaver is so long at the outset of the project, you can't work with the free end. Rather, grasp the weaver fairly close to the secured end and lace it through the warp, creating the first row, and simultaneously trailing the excess through the warp. Here Fred is about to pull the excess through.

the web to the frame, about ½ inch from the corner (closer will give the woven panel a "pulled" corner). Wrap the webbing around the frame to conceal the cut end and the nail.

Weaving is a simple matter of snaking the strand of webbing over and under and over and under the warp strands. The weaver is—at first anyway—a very long piece, so work close to its secured end. Fold it back on itself and snake a double strand through the warp. Then pull through the excess, which is everything up to the free end. The free end is always the last through (not the first). After you have the excess through, go back and tidy up the webbing, flattening each strand in the warp, pulling the weaver up. This done, loop the weaver around the outside of the frame, and head back. On the return course, you will pass over the warp strands you passed under on the previous pass, and vice versa.

On the first weave, you want to tighten the warp, so go over the high side of each warp strand. With each subsequent pass, the tension of the woven surface will increase. When you are finished, the woven surface will be recessed between the frame members, as shown in the *Weaving Section View.* Anchor the last course as you did the end of the warp; that is, work the last strand temporarily aside, loop the free end around the frame and tack it, then move the weaver back to cover and conceal the end and nail.

WEAVING SECTION VIEW

In weaving the panels in the chaise shown, Fred worked—with the frame in the vise—from the top down to about the middle of the frame. Then he turned the frame and worked up to complete the panel. This kept

TIP

A needle-nose pliers makes a good tool for aligning and straightening the webs. It has a pointed tip to worm into the weave without damaging the material, as well as a handle to provide leverage for moving the web. As you can see, the webbing bunches and folds when you push it with the pliers, but you can easily spread it flat again by "spearing" the far edge and pulling it.

the work area of the frame at a comfortable height for him. You can work from the bottom up or the top down, whichever is better for you.

5. Cut the parts for the side frames. From the 4/4 (four-quarter) stock, cut the legs, rails, arms, arm posts, and crosspieces. For everything but the back legs, this is pretty much a rip and crosscut operation. The back legs, however, need to be carefully laid out on a 5-inch-wide board, as shown in the *Back Leg Layout.* Orienting the leg properly on the board is important so that the leg has the maximum strength the wood's grain structure can offer. The back legs can be cut out with a saber saw, though a band saw will do a better job in less time.

With the parts cut, lay out and cut the various laps. See the *Chair Side Frame Joinery* and *Footrest Side Frame Joinery* drawings. Keep in mind that the chair's two side frames are mirror images of each other, not duplicates. Pay attention, too, to which face each lap is cut into. The arm, for example, has the lap for the back leg cut into the outer face, while the lap for the arm post is cut into the inside face. As you did the web frame laps, cut these on the radial arm saw equipped with a dado cutter. The end laps can be cut assembly-line fashion, using stop blocks to help control the size of the cuts.

Even the laps for the lower rails can be positioned with stop blocks.

Lay out and cut the notches in the legs for the cross-pieces next. And while you are at it, round off the foot ends of the two front legs and the four footrest legs. All these cuts can be handled with a saber saw or, better, on the band saw.

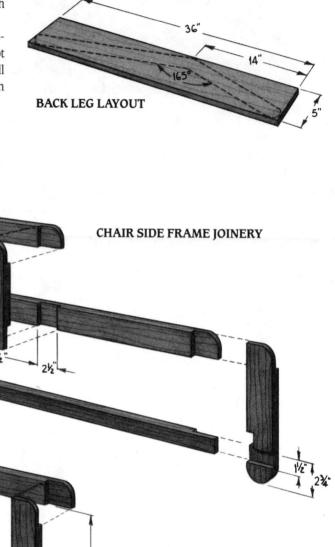

BACK LEG LAYOUT

CHAIR SIDE FRAME JOINERY

FOOTREST SIDE FRAME JOINERY

6. Assemble the side frames. Glue up the side frames of the chair and footrest, pretty much the way you did the web frames. If you cut the laps correctly, the frames should square, but check with a try square and do whatever you can during clamping to keep the frames square. Make sure they are flat, too.

After the clamps are off, cut the corners that must be rounded off—the junction of arm and arm post, of seat rail and front leg, of footrest rail and leg. Use a saber saw. At the same time, trim off any excess at the laps, such as where the arm joins the back leg.

You can ensure good fitting end laps if you cut some of the parts a bit long. The rail joins the back leg, for example, just where it bends. Leaving the rail end square and trimming it flush to the leg's edge after glue-up guarantees a good appearance. Similarly, by cutting a T-lap (such as the arm-to-back-leg joint) as a cross-lap, you can be sure the joint won't slip open during glue-up because it is locked in place mechanically. After the clamps are off, trim off the excess with a saber saw.

7. **Apply a finish.** Sand all the assemblies thoroughly. Using a router and a ¼-inch rounding-over bit, radius the edges of the side frames, inside and out. Dust the frames with a tack cloth to remove all the dust.

Apply two coats of an exterior-grade penetrating oil. The second coat should go on while the first coat is still wet. Give the first coat 15 to 30 minutes to penetrate the wood surface before applying the second.

8. **Assemble the chaise.** We chose to attach the panels to the side frames with showy brass screws, five on each side of the footrest and seat web frames, and three on each side of the back web frame. The screws in the chair sides are fitted with brass finish washers, which make them stand proud of the wood's surface. But with the footrest, such an arrangement would interfere with the sliding action; here the screws are countersunk just enough to make them flush. In each case, drill pilot holes through the side frames and into the web frames.

After the web frames and side frames are assembled, add the crosspieces. These side-to-side members fit into the notches in the lower legs, and they are secured with brass screws driven through the crosspiece into the leg. Install a long crosspiece at the back of the chair and the short crosspiece at the front of the footrest. Slide the foot-

CHAIR-FOOTREST INTERCONNECTION

rest under the chair and install the two remaining long crosspieces. These serve to trap the footrest between the side frames of the chair.

TIP

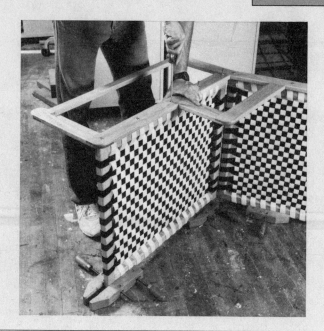

Hand screws can serve as extra hands to help you assemble the web frames between the side frames. Apply two of the wooden-jawed clamps to one side of the backrest frame and two to the side of the seat frame. Stand the frames on the hand screws, as shown. Place the first side frame on them, get the three assemblies properly lined up, then drill pilot holes and drive the screws. With the first side attached, you can turn the assembly over, remove the hand screws, and attach the second side frame.

TERRACE ENSEMBLE

Old-World Charm for Your Terrace

With its classic table and chairs and canvas umbrella, this ensemble would be at home in a formal English garden or outside an Italian villa. The reward of having the ensemble to adorn your terrace equals the challenge of building it.

TERRACE ENSEMBLE TABLE AND CHAIRS

The inspirations for this table and chair set were the various classy and expensive teak outdoor furniture sets that are widely advertised, particularly in mail-order landscaping catalogs. You can't help but admire these handsomely designed, well-crafted pieces.

Because this table and chair set is much more elegant than your run-of-the-mill patio furniture, it deserves special care. Until you're done, you'll have a substantial amount of money and time invested, too much to just plop it on the deck or patio and leave it there through the seasons. Although oak is a durable hardwood and the design is a sturdy one, an outdoor environment takes its toll on any wood furniture, and you'll want to keep this set looking its best. So pick a protected spot for it—under a patio awning or a sundeck trellis, for example—and definitely do not leave it outside all year round.

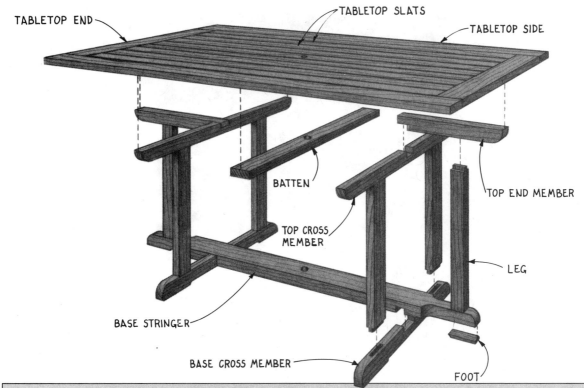

TABLETOP END

TABLETOP SLATS

TABLETOP SIDE

BATTEN

TOP CROSS MEMBER

TOP END MEMBER

LEG

BASE STRINGER

BASE CROSS MEMBER

FOOT

SHOPPING LIST—TABLE

LUMBER
50 bd. ft. 8/4 white oak
42 bd. ft. 5/4 white oak
4½ bd. ft. 4/4 white oak

HARDWARE AND SUPPLIES
1 box #6 × 1⅝" galvanized drywall-type screws
1 box #6 × 2¾" galvanized drywall-type screws
Resorcinol glue

FINISH
Exterior-grade penetrating oil, such as CWF

CUTTING LIST—TABLE

PIECE	NUMBER	THICKNESS	WIDTH	LENGTH	MATERIAL
Top cross members	2	1¾"	2"	34"	8/4 oak
Top end members	2	1¾"	2"	17¾"	8/4 oak
Base stringer	1	1¾"	4"	62"	8/4 oak
Base cross members	2	1¾"	2½"	26"	8/4 oak
Feet	2	¾"	1¾"	5¾"	scrap
Legs	6	1¾"	2½"	24"	8/4 oak
Tabletop ends	2	1"	4"	30"	5/4 oak
Tabletop sides	2	1"	4"	73"*	5/4 oak
Tabletop slats	9	1"	3"	66"	5/4 oak
Batten	1	1"	4"	34"	5/4 oak

*Trim to a finished length of 72" *after* assembly.

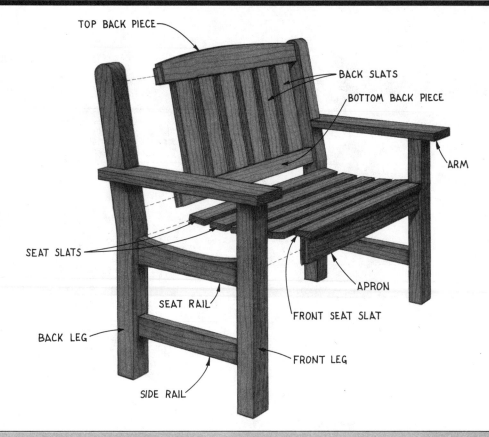

TOP BACK PIECE

BACK SLATS

BOTTOM BACK PIECE

ARM

SEAT SLATS

APRON

SEAT RAIL

FRONT SEAT SLAT

BACK LEG

FRONT LEG

SIDE RAIL

SHOPPING LIST—ARMCHAIR

LUMBER
9¼ bd. ft. 8/4 white oak
6¾ bd. ft. 5/4 white oak
1½ bd. ft. 4/4 white oak

FINISH
Exterior-grade penetrating oil, such as CWF

HARDWARE AND SUPPLIES
1 box #6 × 1⅝" galvanized drywall-type screws
Resorcinol glue

CUTTING LIST—ARMCHAIR

PIECE	NUMBER	THICKNESS	WIDTH	LENGTH	MATERIAL
Front legs	2	1⅞"	2"	23¾"	8/4 oak
Back legs	2	1⅞"	5"	35½"	8/4 oak
Side rails	2	1⅞"	2"	15"	8/4 oak
Seat rails	2	1⅞"	2¾"	15"	8/4 oak
Top back piece	1	1"	3½"	22"	5/4 oak
Bottom back piece	1	1"	2½"	22"	5/4 oak
Back slats	6	¾"	1¾"	14½"	4/4 oak
Apron	1	1"	2½"	22½"	5/4 oak
Seat slats	5	1"	2"	23¾"	5/4 oak
Front seat slat	1	1"	2"	20"	5/4 oak
Arms	2	1"	2¾"	19"	5/4 oak

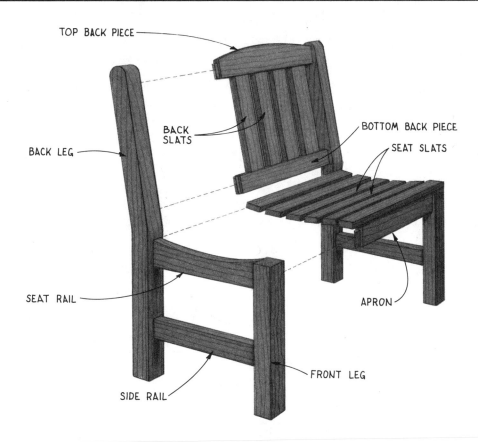

TOP BACK PIECE
BACK SLATS
BACK LEG
BOTTOM BACK PIECE
SEAT SLATS
SEAT RAIL
APRON
SIDE RAIL
FRONT LEG

SHOPPING LIST—CHAIR

LUMBER

8½ bd. ft. 8/4 white oak
3½ bd. ft. 5/4 white oak
1 bd. ft. 4/4 white oak

HARDWARE AND SUPPLIES

1 box #6 × 1⅝" galvanized drywall-type screws
Resorcinol glue

FINISH

Exterior-grade penetrating oil, such as CWF

CUTTING LIST—CHAIR

PIECE	NUMBER	THICKNESS	WIDTH	LENGTH	MATERIAL
Front legs	2	1⅞"	2"	15¾"	8/4 oak
Back legs	2	1⅞"	5"	35½"	8/4 oak
Side rails	2	1⅞"	2"	15"	8/4 oak
Seat rails	2	1⅞"	2¾"	15"	8/4 oak
Top back piece	1	1"	3½"	16¼"	5/4 oak
Bottom back piece	1	1"	2½"	16¼"	5/4 oak
Back slats	4	¾"	1¾"	14½"	4/4 oak
Apron	1	1"	2½"	16¾"	5/4 oak
Seat slats	6	1"	2"	18"	5/4 oak

Builder's Notes

This project is one of our more demanding ones. For the woodworker looking for a challenge, here it is. The basic material is oak, a wood that demands attention from you *before* it's ready to be worked. The principle joint is the mortise and tenon, one that takes practice to master and time to cut and fit, one that many experienced woodworkers avoid. And the work is extensive, with a table and two kinds of chairs listed on the work order. But the result is a gratifyingly handsome set of furniture for the terrace or patio.

The table is rectangular for a reason. Were it square, its leg assembly would be less able to resist wracking. The tabletop would tend to rotate, twisting the legs, spilling the iced tea, disrupting the conversation. So we made the table rectangular.

You can make the chairs with or without arms—both types are covered on the drawings and instructions. Make sure you use the appropriate cutting list for the type you're making because the length of some parts are different. Rather than simply extend the front leg to support the arm, you need to widen the seat also. If you don't, the chair turns out to be too narrow—particularly between the arms—for all but the most slender fannies.

Materials. While teak is the material that comes to mind as the natural choice for this sort of outdoor furniture, we all have (or should have) reservations about using teak. Oak is readily available here in the eastern United States, it looks very good, and white oak is a species that has better than average decay resistance (its relative, red oak, is considerably less decay resistant). So oak is a good choice for this upscale outdoor furniture ensemble, and it is the choice we made.

If you haven't already worked with a hardwood, you'll find that buying the lumber can be a challenge in itself. Hardwoods aren't stocked at every lumberyard. When they are, they are usually stocked in pretty unpredictable dimensions. While thicknesses are standardized, lengths and widths are not. The length is whatever length the log was—nothing is trimmed off to square the board's ends. The width is the maximum the sawyer could eke out of the log. The standard unit—particularly for pricing purposes—is the board foot, a volumetric measure calculated by multiplying the thickness in inches by the width in inches by the length in feet, then dividing the result by 12.

The upshot of all this is that you may have to shop around just to find the species you want. (Phil Gehret, who built the table and chairs, purchased the material, kiln dried, from a local sawmill.) Then, too, you must keep the dimensions of the necessary parts in mind when you shop. Our "Shopping List," specifying so many board feet of such-and-such a thickness, isn't quite good enough. Rather than predetermining that you need so many boards of a particular size, you have to look at what's available and judge which ones will give you the parts you need. It's tricky, because it's easy to misjudge, to forget a couple of key parts, or to overlook a major defect you can't work around. So give yourself some leeway and buy a little extra.

As you close the deal for the wood, consider its state. It is probably rough-sawn. Before you can start cutting parts and joints, the wood has to be reduced to working thicknesses and surfaced to make it smooth and flat. If you have—or have access to—a thickness planer and a jointer, you can do this work yourself. If you don't have these tools, be prepared to pay the lumber dealer to do it for you.

Tools and techniques. As does much fine furniture, this set employs a lot of mortise-and-tenon joinery. Tenons are pretty easy to make; you can cut them with a router, on a table saw, with a radial arm saw, or on a band saw. But mortises are more of a challenge for the hobby woodworker. The standard procedure is to drill a series of holes inside the mortise layout lines to rough it

TOOL LIST

Band saw	Paintbrush
Bar or pipe clamps	Planer
Belt sander	Router
Chisels	¼" rounding-over bit
Clamps	¾" straight bit
Drill	Rubber mallet
Pilot hole bit	Ruler
Drill press	Saber saw
⅜" Forstner bit	Sandpaper
¾" Forstner bit	Saw for crosscutting
⅜" plug cutter	Sawhorses
Countersink bit	Screwdriver
Hollow-chisel mortising	Table saw
attachment	Dado cutter
Finishing sander	Miter gauge
Hand plane	Tack cloth
Hand screws	Tape measure
Hole saw, 1¾"	Try square
Jointer	Yardsticks

out. To do this, you use a bit that's the width of the desired mortise, perhaps 1/16 inch smaller. Then you clean up and square the mortise walls with a chisel.

The holes you bore should be perfectly straight and aligned, and all bored to the same depth. You *can* do the job with a portable electric drill fitted with a 90-degree drill guide, but such contrivances are often clumsy and awkward to use. A drill press will do the job much more quickly and accurately. The holes will be plumb, and you can adjust the machine so the holes will be of a consistent depth. You can mount a fence on the table to help position the mortises. Fitted with a hollow-chisel mortising attachment (that bores square holes), the drill press becomes even more efficient.

When making mortise-and-tenon joints, it's best to cut all the mortises first, then cut the corresponding tenons for an exact fit. Number each joint so you know which tenon fits into which mortise and how they should be oriented.

Making the chairs amounts to a small production run. You need four chairs at minimum, so you are making duplicates of every part. Minimize layout work by using setups effectively, and you'll save time and work. Keep the parts organized and clearly labeled, and you'll save time.

A detailing procedure that crops up again and again in these projects is rounding-over the exposed edges of the parts. It seems to be a signature touch on the part of Fred Matlack and Phil Gehret, Rodale's woodworking project mavens. They radius the edges of everything they build.

It isn't *always* as easy as running the part by the rounding-over bit on the router table, though. In this project, you can deal with the legs and the tabletop slats, among other parts, that way. But you need to be careful where two parts join; here you want the radius on one edge to blend into the radius on the other. The easiest way to achieve this effect, of course, is to machine the edges after assembly. But "easiest" isn't always possible. Sometimes you have to dry assemble joints, mark edges, then disassemble and machine.

It seems like a lot of trouble, but the details often do. Until they pay off in the finished project.

Finish. Unless protected with a finish, oak will weather poorly. It darkens rather dramatically, for example. A clear finish, given the attractiveness—not to say the expensiveness—of the wood, is in order.

For this ensemble, we used CWF, a penetrating oil especially formulated for outdoor use. (CWF, the brand name, stands for Clear Wood Finish.) The theory of the penetrating oil finish is that it, as the name indicates, penetrates the wood's surface and seals it. By keeping standing water—from rain, dew, the lawn sprinkler—from soaking in, the finish minimizes the expansion and contraction that lead to warping, checking, splitting, and joint failure. The finish helps prevent molds and mildew from getting established, and helps keep the wood's natural resins from baking out under the hot sun.

Generally, manufacturers instruct you to brush on the oil liberally, letting it penetrate. And, in fact, when you brush it on you can see it soak into the wood. After 15 minutes to a half-hour, apply more. While these finishes generally are supposed to dry in 24 to 48 hours, in my experience, it often takes three to five days for the solvent smells to dissipate. CWF actually seems to form a surface film as it dries to a matte sheen.

Initially, the finish will darken the wood somewhat. And as the piece weathers, the finish *will* break down and allow the wood to darken and turn silvery-gray. The solution, of course, is to renew the finish every couple of years.

Table

1. Cut and shape the base parts. Cut the two base cross members and the base stringer to the sizes specified by the "Cutting List." Following the *Base Stringer Layout* and the *Base Cross Member Layout,* mark the sizes and locations of the mortises for the legs and the laps that join the three pieces, as well as the final contours.

Cut the laps first, using a router and a straight bit. Though the cross members are thicker than the stringer at this point, bear in mind that after the cross member contours are cut, they'll be the same thickness as the stringer at the laps. Plan to cut the laps a hair undersize, then to refine the fit by paring with a chisel. To prevent tearout that could mar the project, clamp scraps to each

TIP

A Forstner bit bores a clean, flat-bottomed hole, which makes it an excellent bit to use in roughing out mortises. Investing in a couple of sizes—say ⅜ inch and ¾ inch—would enable you to tackle mortise-and-tenon joinery effectively, without incurring the expense of a hollow-chisel mortising attachment.

Next, cut the mortises. If you have a hollow-chisel mortising attachment, use it. If you don't, select a bit that is the same diameter as the width of the mortises, and chuck it in your drill press. Clamp a fence to the drill press table, positioning it so the center point of the bit will enter the centerline of the workpiece. Drill a series of slightly overlapping holes the length of the mortise. Cut the two mortises in the stringer, then reset the fence and rough out the mortises in the cross members. (If possible, maintain the drill press setup for roughing out the top cross member mortises.) With a chisel, pare the sides and ends of the mortises to square them and bring them to their final dimensions.

If you are planning to use an umbrella with the table, cut the hole for its post in the stringer. Use a 1¾-inch hole saw, boring as deep as possible from one side. Then withdraw the cutter, turn the stringer over, and complete the operation from the other side.

The final operation in this step is to cut the contours. Do this on a band saw. After cutting, sand the surfaces to remove saw marks.

side of the workpiece. Then clamp parallel straightedges across the workpiece, positioned to control the width of the lap. Cut each in several passes; oak is pretty hard, and the router is primarily a trimming tool, so don't try to cut more than an additional ⅛ inch with each pass. You can save some time by clamping the two cross members together and lapping both at the same time. After rough-cutting the laps with the router, fit the parts together and refine the width and depth of the laps using a chisel.

BASE STRINGER LAYOUT

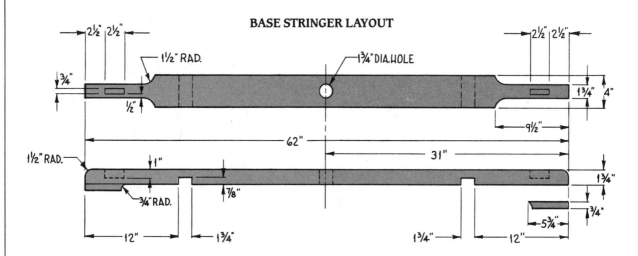

BASE CROSS MEMBER LAYOUT

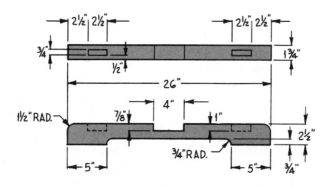

TABLE PLAN VIEWS

TOP VIEW

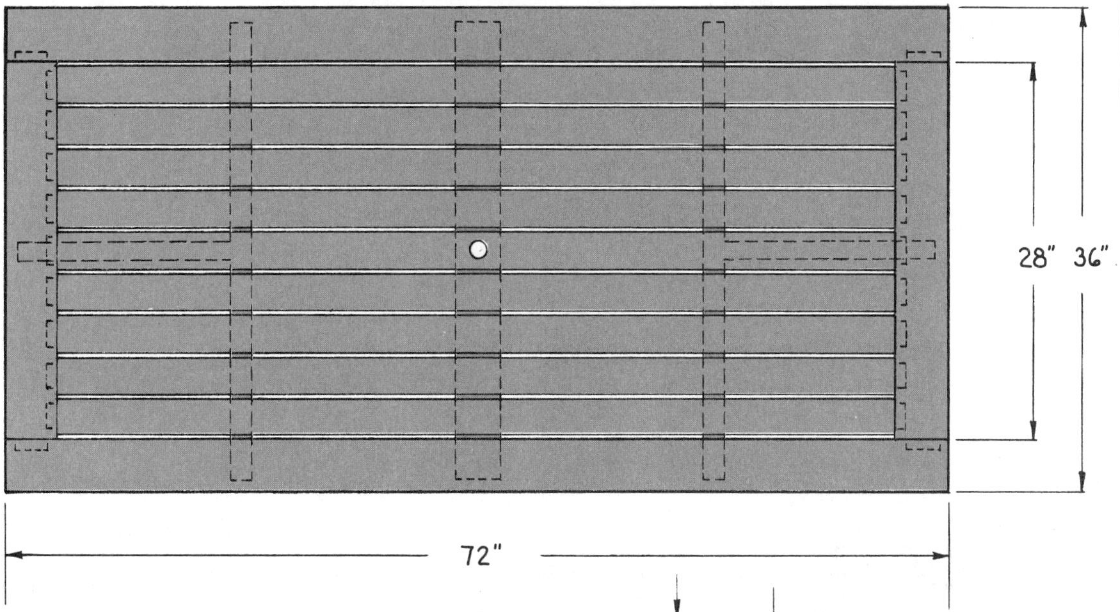

28" 36"

72"

SIDE VIEW

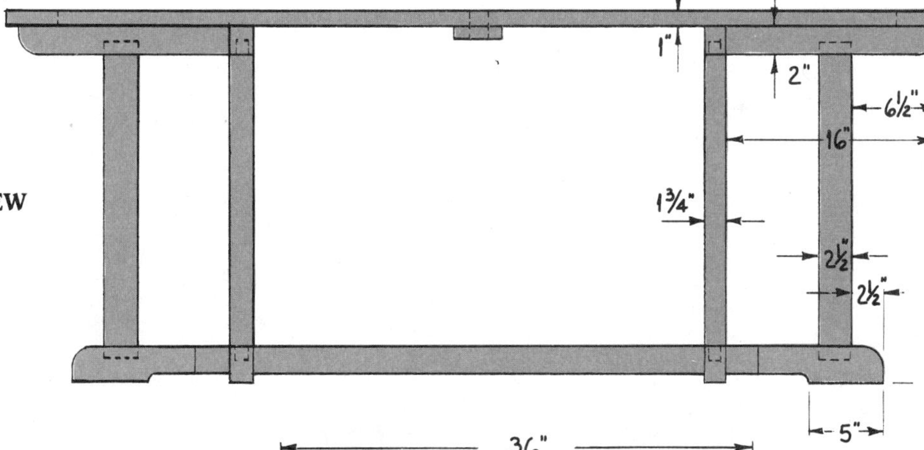

1"

2"

6½"

16"

1¾"

2½"

2½"

5"

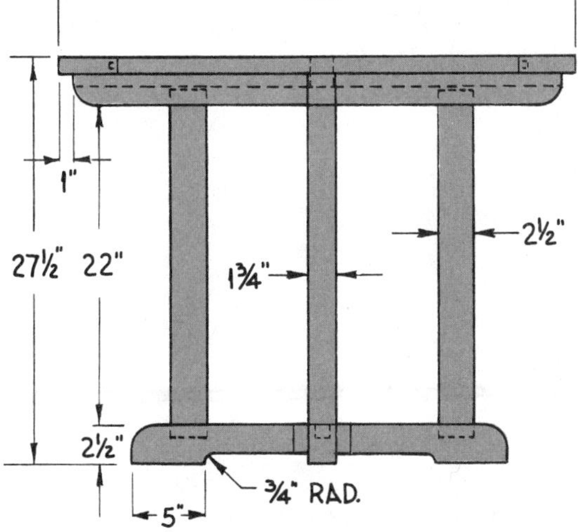

36"

1"

2½"

27½" 22"

1¾"

2½"

¾" RAD.

5"

END VIEW

2. Cut and shape the top members. This step is pretty much a repeat of the previous step, but with different parts. Rough-cut the four top members to the sizes specified by the "Cutting List." Following the *Top Cross Member Layout* and the *Top End Member Layout,* mark the sizes and locations of the laps, mortises, and contours that must be cut.

Cut the laps first, again using a router and straight bit. Remember to clamp scraps on each side of the workpieces to prevent tearout. Remember, too, that you can clamp like parts together and lap both at the same time. And to get the proper fit, rough-cut the laps just a tad undersize, and in a process of alternately test fitting and paring with a chisel, bring them to their final fit.

Cut the mortises next. Since these mortises match those in the base cross members, you can use the same drill press setup to rough them out. Pare them to their final dimensions with a chisel.

Finally, cut the contours of the parts on the band saw, then sand away the tool marks with a belt sander.

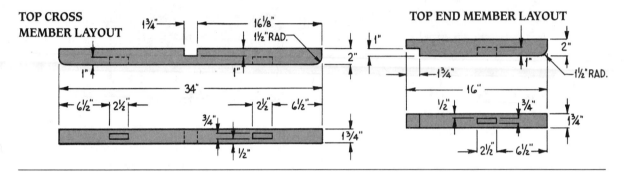

TOP CROSS MEMBER LAYOUT

TOP END MEMBER LAYOUT

3. Assemble the base and top frames. Dry assemble the top frame and the base frame one last time. If the lap joints fit to your satisfaction, glue and screw the parts together. Use resorcinol glue. With the base, drive a couple of 1⅝-inch screws through the bottoms of the cross members into the stringer. With the top frame, drive the same number of screws through the tops of the cross members into the end members.

Cut and glue the feet to the stringer. Cut two scraps to the size specified by the "Cutting List." Set the base assembly on a flat surface, and measure from the bottom of the stringer to the surface. If necessary, plane the feet to that thickness, then glue them to the underside of the stringer at each end. After the glue sets, sand the three frames.

Although the feet are integral to the base cross members, they have to be glued to the base stringer. Because of the size of the stringer, this is an easier and less wasteful approach. After the stringer is joined to the cross members, cantilever an end off the workbench and glue and clamp a foot in place.

4. Cut and tenon the legs. Cut the six legs to the size specified by the "Cutting List."

Each leg is tenoned on both ends, as shown in the *Leg Tenon Detail.* While you can cut the tenons with a router and a straight bit, it probably is easiest to cut them on a table saw with a dado cutter. Set up the dado cutter, and position the rip fence so it is the length of the tenon away from the *outside* of the blade. When the end of the leg is butted against the fence, the blade will cut the tenon's shoulder. Set the depth of cut to give you a tenon that's just a tad fat. Make test cuts on a scrap of the leg stock to confirm the accuracy of your settings. When cutting the tenons, guide the leg with the miter gauge. Make a series of passes; on the last, the butt end of the leg should be against the rip fence. With the saw set up, you can quickly cut tenons on both ends of each leg.

After all the tenons are cut, carefully fit them to particular mortises. On each leg, one tenon has to fit a mortise in a base member, while the other tenon has to fit a mortise in the corresponding top member. Assuming you did cut the tenons a bit thick, use a chisel to pare the tenon's cheeks until an appropriate, snug fit is obtained.

Finally, using a router and a ¼-inch rounding-over bit, radius the edges of the legs.

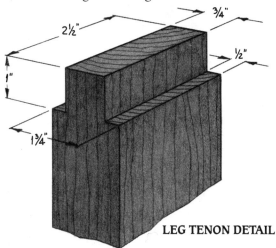

LEG TENON DETAIL

TIP

After paring a tenon to fit a particular mortise, mark both so you don't get them mixed up later. To avoid accidental erasures, chisel Roman numerals (what else?), locating the marks where they'll be concealed after assembly. If you mark surfaces that adjoin when properly assembled, you can indicate the correct orientation of tenon in mortise.

5. Assemble the table base. The radiused edge is a characteristic of virtually all the pieces in this book, and the Terrace Ensemble is no exception. To work all the exposed edges sometimes takes some doing, and with the table, some edges have to be worked before assembly and some after. Before actually gluing the legs to the base and top frames, use the router and a ¼-inch rounding-over bit to radius all the appropriate edges.

Assembly of the table base is a two-person operation. You need to apply glue to both mating surfaces; in this case, the mortise as well as the tenon. Resorcinol glue is runny, and it stains. If you hold the mortises upside down, glue can run out, drip on other parts of the project, and stain them.

Turn the two top frames so the mortises face up. Apply glue to them and to the tenons on the legs. Fit the legs into the top frames. Then apply glue to the lower tenons and the base mortises. With a helper, lift one leg-and-top-frame unit, turn it right-side up, and fit the tenons into the base mortises. Repeat with the second unit.

Dry assemble the table's base to determine which edges—or sections of edges—can be radiused before assembly, and which must wait until after assembly. Make a practice run around the assembly with the router—Be sure it's turned off!—marking starting and stopping points, as above, and determining on which surfaces you'll have to rest the router to get all the spots. While it's easiest to machine individual pieces, you want to blend one part into another where they join, so some edges have to be machined in an assembled state.

(continued)

Apply bar or pipe clamps to hold the parts firmly together. Remember that with resorcinol glue, great pressure is not necessary. Rather, you need to hold the parts together and leave them undisturbed until the glue cures.

Above: The legs can be radiused before assembly. The stringer and cross members are best worked in an assembled state, with the router riding on their top surfaces. *Right:* Where their edges fair into the legs, they have to be worked with the router bearing on their side surfaces.

The most important thing shown in the photos is the sequence necessary to fair the leg and stringer together. The stringer's shape and the router base's diameter dictate that you do part of the stringer with the leg removed, and part with the leg in place. Note also at right that you must block up the assembly to gain clearance when working from the side.

6. **Cut the joinery on the tabletop parts.** Constructed of 5/4 (five-quarter) stock, the tabletop consists of nine 3-inch-wide slats, surrounded by a frame of 4-inch-wide boards. Mortises and tenons are used to join all the pieces together.

Start by cutting all the tabletop parts to the sizes specified by the "Cutting List."

The slats and ends are tenoned on both ends, and the tenons are shouldered on all four sides. Set up the table saw for tenoning by installing the dado cutter; the width

of cut isn't important except to minimize the number of passes required to complete a tenon. Set the depth of cut to 5/16 inch, or just a hair less. Position the rip fence 1 inch from the *outside* of the cutter. When cutting the tenons, guide the workpieces with the miter gauge.

After all the tenons are cut, lay out the mortises on the ends and the sides, following the *Tabletop Joinery* drawing. If cut properly, the sides will be 1 inch longer than their finished length. Lay out the mortises so the extra length is divided, with half at each end.

TABLETOP JOINERY

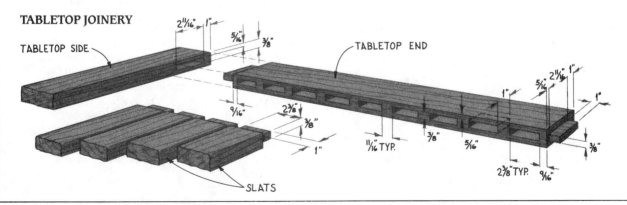

(The extra length serves two purposes here. By making the sides overlong, then trimming them flush with the ends after assembly, you ensure that one won't come up a tad short. Perhaps more important, there's only 5/16 inch of end-grain stock between the mortise and the butt end in the finished piece. Oak splits relatively easily, so having an extra ½ inch of stock there during assembly helps ensure that it doesn't break as you force the tenon in the mortise.)

Now cut the mortises. Since all are centered on the edge of 5/4 stock and all are 3/8 inch wide, set up the drill press with a fence to position the mortises uniformly. Set the depth stop so the mortises will be just over 1 inch deep. Drill out the waste with a 3/8-inch bit, perferably a Forstner bit. Lay out all the parts and mark the joints—which tenon goes into which mortise—then, using a chisel, pare the mortises to accommodate their tenons.

---

7. Assemble the tabletop. Start by dry assembling the tabletop parts. Better to find out now about any problems with fit than after you've mixed and spread the glue. With the parts together, mark on the tabletop sides where the ends meet them.

Knock the assembly apart. With a router and a ¼-inch rounding-over bit, radius the edges of the slats. Radius the inner edges of the sides, too, beginning where one end meets the side and terminating where the other end meets it.

Repeat the assembly process, this time using glue. Capture the slats between the ends, then the ends between the sides. Apply pipe or bar clamps across the top and bottom of the tabletop. Use scrap as cauls between the clamp jaws and the wood to prevent damage.

After the glue sets and the clamps are off, cut and

Although many parts are coming together in precision-fitted joints, assembly of the tabletop is easily a one-person operation. A dry run is advisable; although you may have fit the joints individually, you need to make sure they fit in concert. A dry run is shown here.

Top: Lay out the parts on a benchtop. Align the slats carefully, then position the ends and sides. Note that all the joints are clearly and legibly marked, so each tenon goes into the mortise to which it was fitted. The letters on the tenons should be visible even after a coat of maroon resorcinol is applied, and the markings on the end will be erased by the finish sanding. Cock the tabletop end slightly, so you can progressively align each slat tenon, getting a corner of it into the appropriate mortise. As you move to the next slat and the next, previously started joints will be gradually closed up. Use a rubber mallet, which won't deface the wood. After all the tenons have been started into their mortises, drive the end home.

Repeat the process to install the other tabletop end. Then fit the tabletop sides to the assembly. The sides lock the assembly together, serving to clamp the slats between the ends. In the final gluing-up process, apply bar or pipe clamps across each end of the tabletop.

Bottom: Note the pencil mark on the side piece where the edge radiusing ends; the mark was made in a previous dry fitting, before the edge was routed. Note also that the extra length of the sides—though it is for other purposes—provides a means of dismantling the tabletop after a dry assembly; a mallet blow on the projecting corner will drive the side off its tenons.

attach the batten to the underside of the tabletop, centered across the slats. Drill and countersink pilot holes, then drill a screw through the batten into each side and slat. If you plan to use an umbrella with the table, use a hole saw to cut a pole hole through the center of the top and batten. Work from the top of the table until the hole saw's pilot bit penetrates the batten, then turn the assembly over and complete the hole from the bottom.

Finally, trim the "wild" ends of the sides with a saber saw or circular saw, then radius the outside edges of the tabletop with a router and a ¼-inch rounding-over bit.

---

8. Attach the tabletop to the base assembly. Center the tabletop on the base. With hand screws, clamp the tabletop to the top cross members. Working underneath the table, drill and countersink pilot holes, then drive screws up through the top cross members into each of the slats. Also drive several screws through each of the top end members into the center slat.

---

9. Finish the table. Sand the entire table. As noted in the "Builder's Notes," we used CWF, an exterior-grade penetrating oil. Following the manufacturer's instructions, we brushed on a liberal application, let it soak into the wood for about 20 minutes, then brushed on another coat. We let the finish dry for two or three days before putting the table to use.

Chairs

1. Make templates for laying out the legs, top back piece, and seat rail. Several of the chair parts are involved or judgmental to lay out. To expedite the work, and to keep the parts as uniform as possible (since you'll be making four or more chairs), it's a good idea to make templates for these parts. Use thin plywood, posterboard, or heavy cardboard for the templates.

Prepare a template for the back leg first. On a piece of ¼-inch plywood the size of the leg blank (as specified by the "Cutting List"), mark the outline of the leg, as shown in the *Leg Layouts.* Include the mortises needed for the back assembly. With a saber saw, cut out the template, including the mortises. You will lay this template on the leg blank and trace around it with a pencil, and you need to be able to mark the mortises at the same time.

Do the back top piece and the seat rail templates next. Remember there are two sizes of back top pieces: one for the armchair, and a shortened one for the regular chair. Start with a piece of ¼-inch plywood that is the size of the tenoned blank for the particular part, *excluding* the tenons. Both these parts have a curved edge, and the contour of the curve is up to you (you could even decide you want no curve at all). Assuming you do want a

Make a template for the back legs from plywood or hardboard. Since there are eight back legs to lay out—if you build a set of four chairs—it saves time to lay the leg out once on "template stock," then use the template to lay out the eight legs. Mark the mortise size and locations on the template, then cut "windows" in the template so you can mark the mortises on the stock. The template can then be cut out with a saber saw.

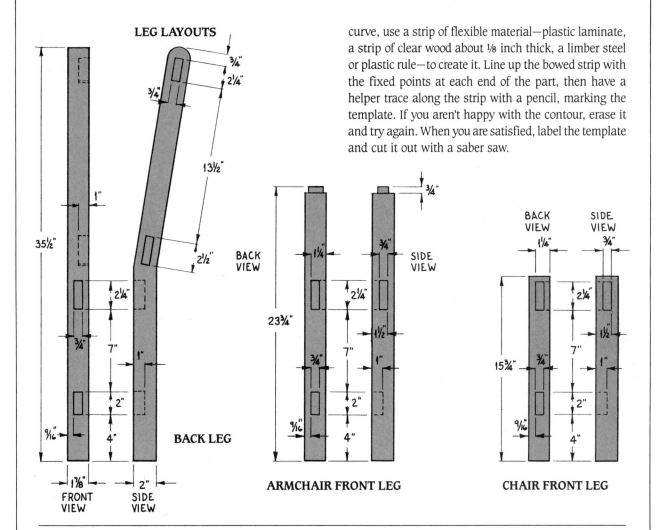

LEG LAYOUTS

3/4"
2 1/4"
3/4"
13 1/2"
2 1/2"
1"
35 1/2"
BACK VIEW
2 1/4"
3/4"
7"
1"
2"
9/16"
4"
BACK LEG
1 7/8"
2"
FRONT VIEW
SIDE VIEW

3/4"
BACK VIEW
SIDE VIEW
1 1/4"
3/4"
2 1/4"
23 3/4"
1 1/2"
3/4"
7"
1"
2"
9/16"
4"
ARMCHAIR FRONT LEG

BACK VIEW
SIDE VIEW
1 1/4"
3/4"
2 1/4"
1 1/2"
15 3/4"
3/4"
7"
1"
2"
9/16"
4"
CHAIR FRONT LEG

curve, use a strip of flexible material—plastic laminate, a strip of clear wood about 1/8 inch thick, a limber steel or plastic rule—to create it. Line up the bowed strip with the fixed points at each end of the part, then have a helper trace along the strip with a pencil, marking the template. If you aren't happy with the contour, erase it and try again. When you are satisfied, label the template and cut it out with a saber saw.

2. **Make the front and back legs.** Cut the front and back legs to the sizes specified by the "Cutting List." If you are duplicating our set, you need eight back leg blanks, two front legs for the armchair, and six front legs for the regular chairs.

Lay out the back legs using the template. Orient the template on the leg blank so both the top and bottom ends align with one edge of the blank and the kink aligns with the opposite edge; this should get the grain direction oriented in the leg for maximum strength (or

Using the template allows you to orient the leg layout quickly. You can try several different orientations, minimizing the impact of defects as much as possible, economizing on materials. Trace around the template and inside the mortise "windows." Keep close stock of the legs you lay out, to ensure that you produce a left and a right for each chair you make.

minimum weakness). Trace around the template, then cut the legs on the band saw. Sand the cut edges smooth.

Do the mortises next. The mortises to be cut into the front and back edges of the legs are all ¾ inch wide and 1+ inches deep, and centered across the stock. Consult the *Leg Layouts* for the length and positioning of the mortises. Remember that you need mirror-image pairs of legs. Laying them out in pairs will help ensure you get the required lefts and rights.

Chuck a ¾-inch bit in the drill press—a Forstner bit is particularly good for this sort of work, since it cuts a clean-sided, flat-bottomed hole. Clamp a fence to the

ARMCHAIR PLAN VIEWS

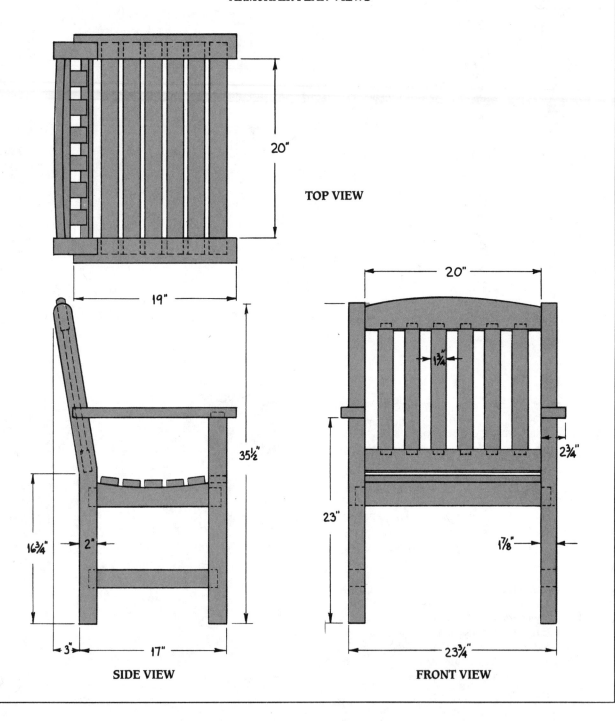

20"

TOP VIEW

19"

20"

1¾"

2¾"

35½"

23"

1⅞"

16¾"

2"

3"

17"

23¾"

SIDE VIEW

FRONT VIEW

drill press table, positioned to center the rough mortise across the width of the leg as much as possible. (You can then perfect the centering by drilling out each mortise, then turning the workpiece around and drilling it again with the opposite side against the fence.)

With the drill press set up in this way, you can

TIP

To set a fence on the drill press for mortising, bore a hole dead center in a length of the leg stock. It may taken several tries to get the hole accurately positioned. When you have The Hole, lower the bit into the hole with the motor turned off and lock the quill. Butt the fence board against the leg stock and clamp it.

CHAIR PLAN VIEWS

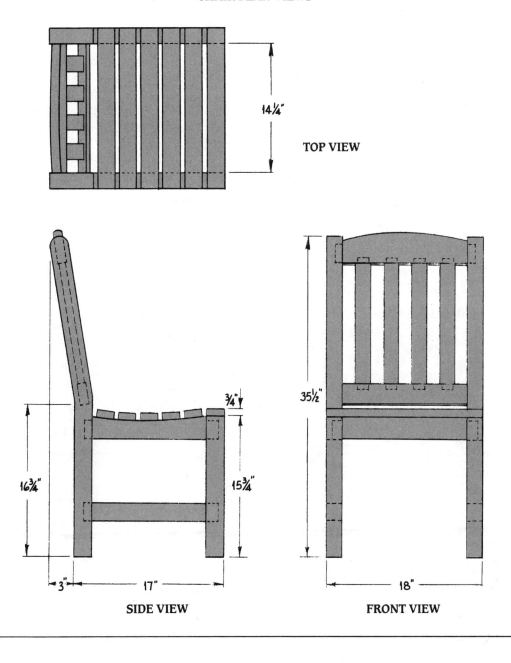

TOP VIEW

SIDE VIEW

FRONT VIEW

simplify mortise layout: Just mark the ends of the mortises, and the setup will establish the sides. Line up the leg blanks side by side. Mark the ends of the mortises on one leg, then use a square to extend them across the lot.

Rough out the seat and side rail mortises in the back legs first. If need be, cut a block from scrap to support the leg on the drill press table while you rough out the mortise closest to the kink. Then, rough out the same mortises in the front legs, and the back mortises in the back legs. After adjusting the fence position, rough out the apron mortises in the front legs. (You need to adjust the fence position because the legs are wider than they are thick.) As you cut these mortises, you'll notice that they break through into the mortises for the seat rails. Square up the mortises with a chisel, removing the ridges left by the round drill bit.

3. Cut and tenon the rails, aprons, and back parts. The most efficient way to produce these parts is to cut them all to size, then to rough out all the tenons. Refining the tenons and cutting the arcs in the seat rails and the top back pieces will be done later. For now, just cut the parts to the sizes specified by the "Cutting List." Since four chairs will require stacks of parts—as many as 18 back slats, for example—be sure to label each piece as it leaves the saw, and make room for tidy stacks, one for each kind of part.

Next, cut tenons on both ends of each of these pieces. All of the tenons are cut using a table saw equipped with a dado cutter; it makes sense to maximize your use of the setup. As you did in other tenoning operations on this project, use the rip fence as a stop to set the tenon length. Set the depth of cut carefully, and test your setting on scraps of the working stock before cutting good parts. And always guide the workpiece over the dado cutter using the miter gauge.

- On the seat and side rails, cut tenons ¾ inch thick and 1 inch long, shouldered on two sides.
- On the aprons, top back pieces, and bottom back pieces, cut tenons ¾ inch thick and 1 inch long, also shouldered on two sides. NOTE that this stock is thinner than the rails, so reduce the depth of cut to get the desired tenon thickness.
- On the back slats, cut tenons ⅜ inch thick and ½ inch long. Shoulder them on all four sides.

The final operation is to cut the tenon on each front leg of the armchair that joins the leg to the arm.

4. Assemble the side frames. Begin this process by matching sets of parts—a front and a back leg with a side and a seat rail. Then pair these sets of parts to make up chairs, adding to each chair an apron and all the parts for a back assembly. Mark each part, so you know which side frame and which chair it is for. Check carefully to ensure each chair will have a left and a right side frame.

Fit the rail tenons to their mortises next. Fit the side rails first. Pare the tenons with a chisel until a snug fit is attained.

Do the seat rails next. Each seat rail tenon must be shortened by cutting away ½ inch of it, forming a shoulder across the top. The front tenon must be mitered, as shown in the *Rail- and Apron-to-Leg Detail,* so it doesn't prevent the apron tenon from seating in its mortise. Both of these refinements can be made on the band saw. At the same time, you can also cut the concave arc for the seat. Use the template you made to

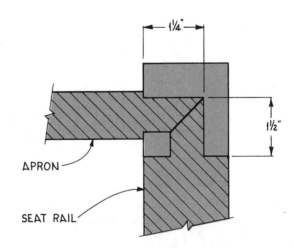

RAIL- AND APRON-TO-LEG DETAIL

lay this out. After cutting the rail, pare the tenons until they fit their respective mortises.

After dry assembling a frame to check how all the joints fit, apply resorcinol glue to mortises and tenons, assemble the frame, and apply clamps. Use scrap cauls between the clamp jaws and the wood to prevent damage. Be sure the frame is flat, not wracked or twisted. Con-tinue this process until all the frames are assembled.

After the glue has set and the clamps are removed, radius all exposed edges with a router and a ¼-inch rounding-over bit.

5. Assemble the backs. Although the back slats have been tenoned, there are no mortises in the tops and bottoms for them to fit into. Lay out the mortises, as shown in the *Back Assembly Joinery* drawing. Rough out the mortises on the drill press, then square them with a chisel. While you are working with the chisel, fit the slat tenons to their mortises.

Now, before going any further, use the template for the top back pieces and lay out the convex arc on each top. Cut them on the band saw, then sand the edges smooth. With a router and a ¼-inch rounding-over bit, radius the top (curved) edges of the tops and the bottom edges of the bottoms. Radius all the edges of the slats.

Fit the tenons on the tops and bottoms to their mortises in the back legs. Then, to be sure the tenons will fit their mortises when the slats are in place, assemble each back unit without glue, both to finalize the fit of all the joints together, and to test the fit to the legs. When you are satisfied with the way everything fits, glue up each back assembly. Again, protect the wood from clamp damage with cauls. And be sure each back is flat and square.

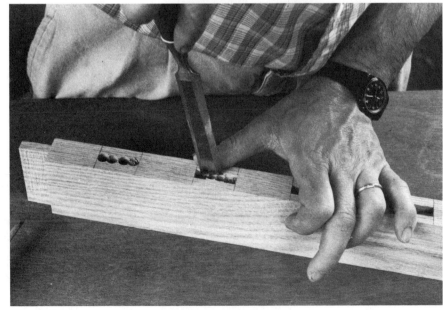

One operation—squaring the roughed-out mortises—performed two ways: cutting with a chisel and shop-made mallet, and paring. In either case, the mortise has been roughed out with a drill bit in a drill press. The pencil marks across the workpiece indicate the "ends" of the mortise. The sides are established by the drill press setup, while the bit diameter matches the mortise width. The ridges between the holes need to be removed, the sides pared flat, and the corners squared.

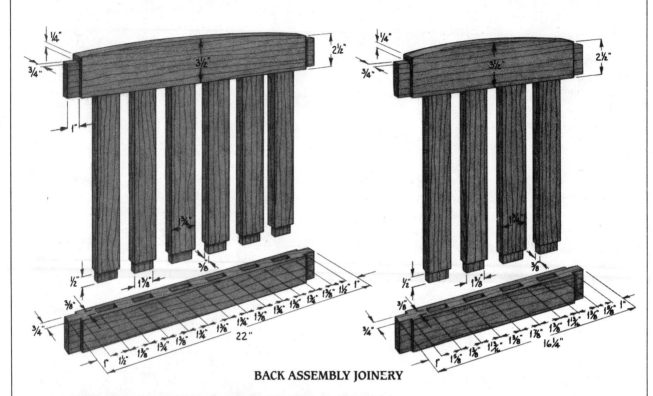

BACK ASSEMBLY JOINERY

If you are making several chairs—and you are—it is worthwhile to make a template of the back's curve and trace it onto the workpieces. Note that the mortises and the tenons have already been cut—done while the piece is square.

6. Assemble the chairs. Connect the two side frames at the back with the back assembly and at the front with the apron to form the chair frame. You should already have assured yourself that the back assemblies fit their respective side frames. You still have to fit the apron, however.

On the band saw, miter the end of the apron tenons, as you did the tenons on the seat rails. Also cut away ½ inch of the tenon height, forming a shoulder across the top of the tenon. If necessary, pare each tenon

with a chisel to fit it to its mortise. Finally, radius the bottom edges with a router and a ¼-inch rounding-over bit.

After dry assembly has assured you the parts fit satisfactorily, glue them together. Apply clamps overnight; you can use bar or pipe clamps, or you can wrap a band clamp around the assembly. In any case, remember that great pressure is not going to improve the set of the resorcinol glue, so don't invest more effort here than is necessary.

7. Cut and install the seat slats. Cut the seat slats to the sizes specified by the "Cutting List." The slats for the regular chair are uniformly sized, but the armchair requires two different lengths. Radius the two exposed edges of each.

Attach five slats to the seat rail, spacing the slats equally. Attach the sixth slat to the front legs and apron. On the armchair, the front slat is shorter than the others and fits between the front legs; it is attached to the apron. Use glue and 1⅝-inch galvanized screws, driving the screws into counterbored pilot holes.

For a finished appearance, conceal the screw heads with wooden plugs, which you glue into the counterbores. Use a plug cutter—match it to the diameter of the counterbores—to cut the plugs from scrap stock.

8. Cut and attach the arms to the armchair. Cut the arms to the size specified by the "Cutting List." Radius the edges with a router and a ¼-inch rounding-over bit. Notch the back end of the arm to fit around the back leg. Lay out and cut the mortise for the front leg tenon.

Attach the arm by fitting the mortise onto the tenon, aligning the back end so the arm is level, and driving a screw through the edge of the arm into the back leg. Lock the arm on the leg tenon with a screw driven through the edge of the arm into the tenon. Counterbore both pilot holes, and cover the screws with wooden plugs.

9. Finish the chairs. Sand the chairs carefully. Apply two coats of an exterior-grade penetrating oil. Apply the second coat while the first coat is still wet, about 15 to 30 minutes after the initial application.

TERRACE ENSEMBLE UMBRELLA

This umbrella has been a big hit with everyone who has seen it. Though it looks devilishly complicated, it is quite simple to build, because it is cleverly done. It just takes time. Sewing the cover may be the most difficult part of the project.

The inspiration for the Terrace Umbrella was the Italian market umbrellas, which sell for about $500 to $700 a pop. A base costs extra, of course. Fred Matlack, who designed and built our Terrace Umbrella, estimates that his version has less than $100 in materials in it, including the fabric for the cover and the oak for the base.

The umbrella uses a relatively small amount of oak, ripped into a pole and many slender arms and struts. But it requires (what seems like) a couple of pounds of hardware—angle plates, *lots* of picture hangers, some S-hooks, screws, and machine screws with locknuts.

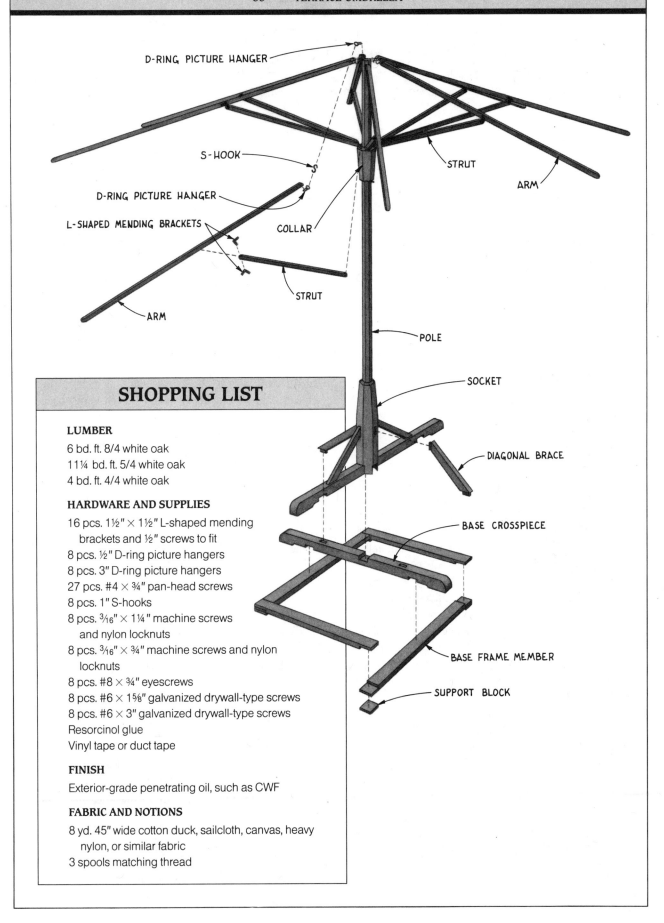

D-RING PICTURE HANGER

S-HOOK

D-RING PICTURE HANGER

L-SHAPED MENDING BRACKETS

COLLAR

STRUT

ARM

STRUT

ARM

POLE

SOCKET

DIAGONAL BRACE

BASE CROSSPIECE

BASE FRAME MEMBER

SUPPORT BLOCK

SHOPPING LIST

LUMBER

6 bd. ft. 8/4 white oak
11¼ bd. ft. 5/4 white oak
4 bd. ft. 4/4 white oak

HARDWARE AND SUPPLIES

16 pcs. 1½" × 1½" L-shaped mending
  brackets and ½" screws to fit
8 pcs. ½" D-ring picture hangers
8 pcs. 3" D-ring picture hangers
27 pcs. #4 × ¾" pan-head screws
8 pcs. 1" S-hooks
8 pcs. $\frac{3}{16}$" × 1¼" machine screws
  and nylon locknuts
8 pcs. $\frac{3}{16}$" × ¾" machine screws and nylon
  locknuts
8 pcs. #8 × ¾" eyescrews
8 pcs. #6 × 1⅝" galvanized drywall-type screws
8 pcs. #6 × 3" galvanized drywall-type screws
Resorcinol glue
Vinyl tape or duct tape

FINISH

Exterior-grade penetrating oil, such as CWF

FABRIC AND NOTIONS

8 yd. 45" wide cotton duck, sailcloth, canvas, heavy
  nylon, or similar fabric
3 spools matching thread

CUTTING LIST

PIECE	NUMBER	THICKNESS	WIDTH	LENGTH	MATERIAL
Umbrella					
Pole	1	1½"	1½"	96"	8/4 oak
Struts	8	½"	¾"	30"	4/4 oak
Arms	8	1"	1½"	56"	5/4 oak
Collar segments	8	1"	1½"	8"	5/4 oak
Umbrella Base (optional)					
Socket segments	8	1"	1½"	20"	5/4 oak
Base crosspieces	2	1⅞"	2⅜"	42"	8/4 oak
Diagonal braces	4	1"	1⅞"	16"	5/4 oak
Base frame members	4	¾"	1⅞"	30"	4/4 oak
Support blocks	4	½"	1⅞"	1⅞"	4/4 oak

Builder's Notes

Although it looks amazingly complex to build, you don't have to be a veteran woodworker to make the umbrella frame and optional umbrella base—the building techniques are pretty straightforward. But it will take more than a few hours to fashion all the parts and assemble them.

The umbrella consists of three elements: the frame, the base, and the fabric cover. The frame consists of a pole, eight arms that hang from the pole top, and eight struts that link the arms to a collar that slides up and down the pole. The engineering design requires the struts to ride against the pole, so when the umbrella is opened, the stress is on the strut and the pole. The cover consists of eight triangular panels that are stitched together. The cover has pockets that fit over the ends of the arms and secure it on the frame. You need the base if you plan to use the umbrella alone, rather than as a sunshade for the ensemble's table and chairs.

Materials. The frame and the base are made of white oak. If you are building just the umbrella, it may be worthwhile for you to skim through the "Builder's Notes" accompanying the Terrace Table and Chairs project on page 18. Information on buying oak is there.

Although the frame doesn't use much wood in its construction, it does use a lot of hardware, all of which should be available at a good hardware store. The photos and drawings that illustrate the construction of the umbrella show what the various hardware bits look like. And, of course, the "Shopping List" tells how many of each piece you should buy.

One interesting bit of hardware used in the frame is the stop nut. It has a nylon insert that keeps the nut in position, even when it isn't jammed tight. This is particularly useful where the screw onto which the nut is threaded is serving as a pivot. The elements being hinged can be given adequate operating clearance without the fear that the nut will work off the screw. In the case of the umbrella, the struts can be left loose enough to pivot easily.

Tools and techniques. The tools used to make the umbrella aren't unusual, and the techniques used add up to standard woodworking. The one stumper was the sliding collar. How to make it—gluing up beveled strips—came easily. How to shape it came hard. Throughout much of the construction, Fred worked with a short blocky collar, which is seen in a number of the procedural photos. The obvious solution to its ungainly appearance was to taper it, but how? Doing it on the jointer would be too hazardous, on the band saw, too complicated. The hand plane was the solution.

Sewing. Making the fabric umbrella cover requires only basic sewing skills. Fred Matlack stitched up the cover shown using a typical home sewing machine. A heavy-duty commercial model isn't required. The cover is, however, a daunting project if you've never used a sewing machine before.

The umbrella shown has a cover made of duck, a cotton fabric. It isn't too heavy, but it isn't waterproof either. For our purposes, that seems fine, since the umbrella is intended to shade you from the sun, rather than shield you from the rain. Sailcloth or a lightweight canvas would be a good choice. They are heavier than the duck; while that makes them more durable, it also makes them more demanding to sew.

TOOL LIST

Band saw
Belt sander
Chisel
Clamps
Drill
   3/16" dia. bit
   1/2" dia. bit.
   Pilot hole bit
Finishing sander
Hand plane
Jack plane
Jointer
Paintbrush
Planer
Router
Router, table-mounted
   1/4" rounding-over bit
   3/4" straight bit
Rubber mallet
Ruler
Sandpaper
Saw for crosscutting
Sawhorses
Screwdriver
Sewing machine
Snug hand clamp
Steel square
Table saw
   Dado cutter
   Miter gauge
Tack cloth
Tape measure
Try square
Vise
Wrenches

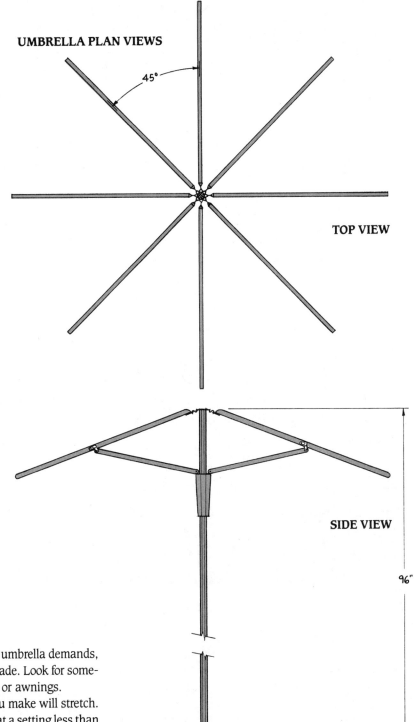

UMBRELLA PLAN VIEWS

45°

TOP VIEW

SIDE VIEW

96"

If canvas is what you feel your umbrella demands, consider seriously having a cover made. Look for someone who makes and sells draperies or awnings.

Bear in mind that the cover you make will stretch. Fred fitted the cover to the umbrella at a setting less than fully open, knowing that it would stretch. He didn't want it to end up too loose and billowy. The first few times the umbrella was opened fully, the fabric was taut, but, as you can see in the photo, it now has a loose, casual appearance.

Note: All the photos show the proper procedure, but some of them reflect the development process. For example, the sliding collar was originally short and straight. The photos depicting the gluing-up process, the installation of the struts, and the drilling of the support-pin holes in the pole all show the original collar. Afterwards, Fred made a second, longer, tapered collar, which is seen in the photo of the finished umbrella.

Umbrella Frame

1. **Make the umbrella pole.** Start by cutting the pole blank to the dimensions specified by the "Cutting List."

The pole must be cut to an octagonal shape, with each face ⅝ inch wide. You can use a band saw or jointer to accomplish this, but we did it on the table saw. Clamp an expendable board to the rip fence to protect it and the blade. Retract the blade, tilt it to 45 degrees, turn the saw on, and carefully raise the blade until it just cuts into the fence. On a scrap the same thickness as the workpiece, make a test cut and measure the width of the cut face. If it is less than ⅝ inch wide, the fence is too close to the blade. If it is more than ⅝ inch wide, the fence is too far away from the blade. Adjust the fence's position accordingly. When you've got the setup, cut the pole.

Note: This setup is something of a compromise. You do have to remove the saw guard, but the top of the blade is buried in the fence facing at all times, and the workpiece covers the blade through most of the cut, protecting the fingers. The compromise is kickback of the waste. The waste will be trapped between the blade and the fence, and will get hurled back. Be forewarned and stand well to the side, so you don't get speared.

An alternative setup would be to feed the work between the blade and the fence. That would eliminate the kickback, but would expose a sizable portion of the blade throughout the cut. Moreover, with this alternative setup, the workpiece would be ruined if it drifted from the fence.

When the pole is completed, sand it smooth and apply two coats of an exterior-grade penetrating oil.

Rip a ⅝-inch-wide chamfer along each edge of the pole blank to form an octagonal pole. Cut the chamfers by clamping an auxiliary wood fence to the fence of the table saw, setting the blade to 45 degrees, and raising it (with the saw running) just into the board, as shown. Cut test chamfers on a scrap of the correct thickness and adjust the fence (retracting the blade each time you move the fence, then resetting it) until the saw cuts a ⅝-inch-wide chamfer. Then cut the pole. **Caution:** When cutting chamfers with this setup, the waste pieces tend to kick back, so don't stand directly behind the blade.

2. **Make the struts and arms.** Cut the eight struts to the dimensions specified by the "Cutting List." Study the *Strut Layout.* Cut a ³⁄₁₆-inch-wide by ¾-inch-deep slot in one end of each strut, then drill a ³⁄₁₆-inch-diameter hole through both ends. Round off the ends last. You can do this with a saber saw or on a band saw, but it may be easiest to stack and clamp the struts in a vise, then freehand a rounded profile on the ends with a belt sander. By stacking the struts, you'll get a fairly uniform profile on all of them. The purpose here is not to duplicate a perfect radius, but to create a smooth curve that will index smoothly against the pole and arm as the umbrella is raised and lowered.

Next, cut the arms to the dimensions specified by the "Cutting List." Study the *Arm Layout.* Line up all eight arms on their sides and pencil an alignment mark across them, 28 inches from the "pole end." Roll them over and duplicate the mark on the opposite face. Round off the pole ends, as shown, and taper and round the outer ends. As you did with the struts, stack and clamp the arms in a vise, then work them with a belt sander. The idea is to soften the profiles, not duplicate a specific shape.

Do any necessary touch-up sanding on both the struts and the arms, then apply two coats of an exterior-grade penetrating oil.

When the finish is dry, mount two L-shaped mending brackets on each arm. The top holes in the brackets should be aligned to accept the bolt that will fasten the strut to the arm.

Finally, fasten the 3-inch D-ring picture hangers to the pole end of the arms using pan-head screws.

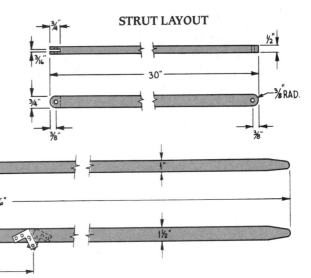

STRUT LAYOUT

ARM LAYOUT

When attaching the mending brackets to the arms—one to each side—orient them so the holes for the strut-mounting bolt are aligned but the bracket-mounting screws are offset. Note that the bolt hole is aligned with the pencil mark on the arm, and that the outside corner of the bracket is flush with one edge of the arm and the inside end corner with the other edge. When the time comes, you'll be able to slip a machine screw through the brackets and struts.

TIP

Use a tenoning jig on your table saw to cut the slots in the struts. The blade will produce the required 3/16-inch slot in two passes, simultaneously centering the slot across the width of the strut.

The typical shop-made tenoning jig—see the plan—straddles the rip fence and has a fixed stop against which to clench (or, better, clamp) the workpiece. When positioning the fence, measure from the face of the jig to the blade. The depth of the slot is determined, of course, by the depth-of-cut setting on the table saw.

In this application, stand the strut on end, side against the jig, locked against the stop. Push the jig along the fence, passing the strut over the blade. Turn the strut 180 degrees and make a second pass. This will bring the slot to the full width desired, and ensure that you have the same thickness of stock on either side of the slot.

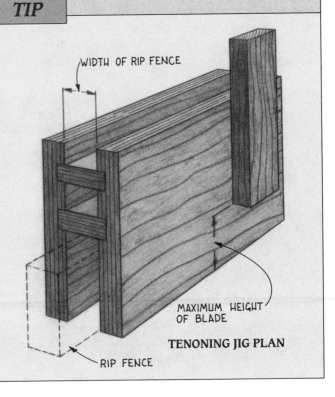

TENONING JIG PLAN

3. **Make the collar.** The collar is made up of eight segments that, when glued up, form an octagonal tube to fit over the pole. Sized properly, the collar should be just loose enough to move up and down the pole freely. As you can see from some of the how-to photos, the basic collar is pretty blocky. So once the collar is glued up, you'll want to plane it to a tapered shape.

Begin by studying the *Collar Detail.* It is easiest to cut uniform segments if you bevel one length of stock, then crosscut the eight segments from it. Rip the stock to the size specified by the "Cutting List," then bevel the edges, as indicated in the drawing, at 22½ degrees. You can rip the bevels on the table saw, using a setup similar to that used to chamfer the umbrella pole. Crosscut the segments to length.

To assemble the collar, lay the segments side by side on two strips of tape, as shown in the photo. Plastic tape is best, because it has some elasticity, but duct tape, masking tape, or any other tape will do. Before applying glue, roll up the segments and tape the bundle. Now you can test how it fits on the pole: It must be loose enough to slide easily, but without excessive play. You decide what "excessive" is; it's your umbrella. If the collar is too tight, cut new segments. Too loose, plane them a little. When the fit is satisfactory, open up the bundle, apply glue to each mating face, then reroll the bundle.

When the glue dries, use a hand plane to taper the collar to the final dimensions. Because the collar is fully tapered, you need to cut a couple of scrap-wood wedges to help secure it in the vise after the first two or three facets are tapered. An alternative approach is to butt the

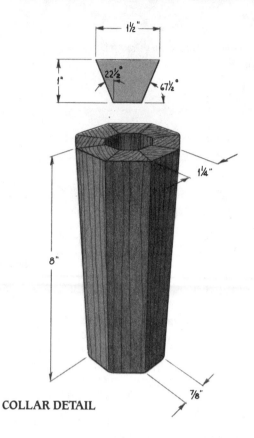

COLLAR DETAIL

collar's bottom end against a bench dog, then clamp it to the benchtop with a speed clamp or C-clamp, the clamp's jaw inside the collar. After the collar is suitably tapered, radius the top and bottom edges with a rounding-over bit in a table-mounted router.

Do any touch-up sanding that is necessary, then apply two coats of an exterior-grade penetrating oil.

TIP

To truss up the sliding collar while the glue set, we used a Snug band clamp. It is a ½-inch-wide strip of mildly elastic plastic. When you buy it (Woodcraft Supply, 210 Wood County Industrial Park, P.O. Box 1686, Parkersburg, WV 26102-1686 is the only source we know of, by the way), you get a 20-foot piece, but you can cut it into somewhat shorter lengths. Just wrap the band tightly around and around the collar. When you get to the last loop, wrap the band over your thumb, as shown, so you can tuck the free end under the band. Pull out your thumb, and the band pinches the end.

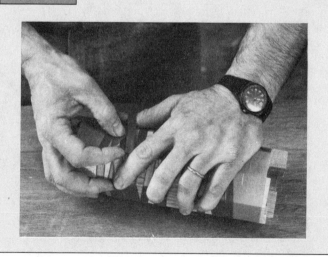

Assembling the sliding collar. Cut the eight pieces and lay them on two pieces of tape, as shown. With the tape linking them together, the segments roll right up in proper alignment. The excess tape wraps around, keeping them bundled. Thus dry assembled, you can test the collar's fit on the pole. If it is okay, peel back the tape, unroll the bundle, and spread glue on the mating surfaces.

4. **Attach the struts to the collar.** Each strut is connected to the sliding collar by a ¾-inch machine screw run through an eyescrew. The idea is to have the strut actually ride against the pole, so the stresses are transferred directly from the strut to the pole, not to the collar. The eyescrews need to be positioned so that happens.

It works best to install one strut at a time. Drill a pilot hole, then turn an eyescrew into place. Slip the strut's slot over the eyescrew, insert the screw, and secure it with a stop nut. Remember that the stop nut will hold its position on the screw without being jammed tight, so the strut can be allowed to pivot freely. Repeat the process until all the struts are installed.

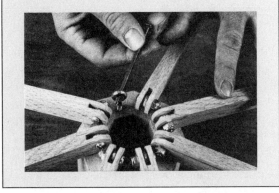

TIP

Working space is at a premium, and it is tough to get good leverage on the eyescrews. Use a 10d nail as a lever.

The last strut is tricky to install. To provide working room for your screwdriver, you need to align the last eyescrew almost parallel to one of its neighbors. After the screw is set, you simply twist the strut into proper position.

5. **Attach the arms to the top of the pole.** Each arm is attached to the pole with two D-ring picture hangers and an S-hook. One hanger is attached to the arm (this you've already done), and the other to the top of the pole. Snag each ring in a loop of the S-hook, then crimp the loops closed.

The first step in doing this is to fasten the eight hangers to the top of the pole. It's really much easier than it looks. Drill a pilot hole in the very center of the top of the pole. Run one pan-head screw through the top holes of all eight hangers, driving it partway into the pilot hole. Because all eight arms will be attached to this one screw, the stresses on it will be equalized, thus minimizing the chance that the pole will split.

Spread the hangers out around the pole-top, arranging a D-ring picture hanger over each flat. Drive a pan-head screw through each hanger and tighten it. Drill a pilot hole for each screw, of course. Finally,

tighten the center screw.

Attach the arms next. Crimp an S-hook onto each arm's D-ring. Then hook an arm onto each D-ring on the pole, crimping it in place. It helps to clamp the pole in a vise while you do this.

The top of the pole is congested with hardware. The center screw is the first one started, the last one tightened. It penetrates all eight picture hangers, so that the stresses are equalized around it, preventing the pole from splitting. Start that first screw, then arrange the connectors so one D-ring is aligned with each flat on the pole. Drive an additional screw through each connector, then tighten the center screw.

TIP

When crimping the S-hooks, use locking-grip pliers. The jaws of these pliers can be preset; they'll snap to that setting when the handles are squeezed. You can thus give each S-hook a uniform crimp (if such details are important to you).

6. Complete the umbrella frame. Join the pole-arm assembly to the collar-strut assembly. To do this, secure the collar in a vise with the struts splayed out around it. Slide the pole into it. One by one, align the struts between the mounting brackets on the arms and bolt them in place. Again, use machine screws and stop nuts.

Finally, drill a series of holes through the pole for a support pin. You push the collar up the pole, insert a pin in a hole, then let the collar settle back onto the pin. While you could pick the setting you like and drill a hole at that setting only, you'll get a better umbrella if you have several stops leading up to the maximum opening.

Left: Link strut and arm with a machine screw and stop nut. The engineering of the umbrella is pretty clear here: The weight of the umbrella is transferred from the arms to the struts through direct contact. The assembly bolts serve merely as pivot points, not as weight bearers.

Right: To select positions for support-pin holes, you can work with a ruler and pencil, or you can be more direct. With the pole secured in a vise, slide the collar up the pole. When the setting "looks right," drill a hole. In any case, make a range of holes.

Umbrella Base

The design of the base puts eight feet on the ground to virtually eliminate tippiness. There are two main crosspieces cross-lapped together. These provide four of the feet. Next, a secondary framework is half-lapped together and fitted to the bottom of the first structure.

Now you have eight feet on the ground. A socket is added to accept the umbrella pole.

Build the eight-footed base first, then make the socket and fit it to the base. Finally, add the diagonal braces.

1. Prepare the stock. Unless you have purchased surfaced stock, prepare your lumber for use, jointing and planing it to reduce it to working thicknesses and to smooth the faces and edges. As you work, it is often productive to crosscut the various parts to a rough length, which is about an inch or two longer than the size specified by the "Cutting List." Be sure you label these pieces. Don't do too much to size the stock for the socket until you are ready to bevel-rip the segments.

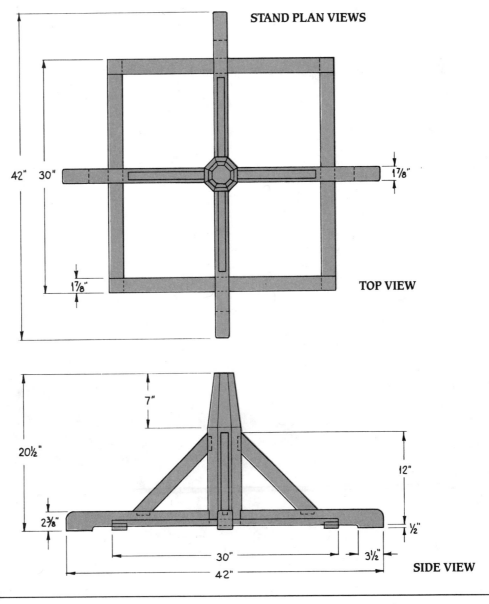

STAND PLAN VIEWS

TOP VIEW

SIDE VIEW

2. Make the crosspieces. Cut the crosspieces to the final dimensions specified by the "Cutting List." Lay out the recess in the bottom edge that forms the feet. (See the *Stand Side View.*) Cut the recesses on the band saw.

Cut the cross-lap joint that connects the two cross-pieces. Cutting the laps with a router and straight bit may be the least problematic approach. If you work on the table saw with a dado cutter, the two members are effectively different thicknesses because of the recesses that form the feet, so you need to lay out the laps fully and work carefully.

3. Make the secondary frame. Cut (or trim) the four secondary frame members to size, then cut half-lap joints at each end of each piece. Assemble the members to form a square frame, as shown in the *Stand Top View*. As you glue up this assembly, be sure the frame is square and flat.

Without glue, assemble the two crosspieces, and turn the assembly upside down on a flat surface. Position the secondary frame on it, also upside down. Mark where the frame members intersect the crosspieces, scribing along both sides of each frame member on the crosspieces. Notch the crosspieces to accept the frame; the scribed lines delineate the shoulders of the notches. You won't be able to cut these notches (or laps) with a router, because of their proximity to the feet, so cut them on the table saw with a dado cutter. All are cut at the same depth-of-cut setting.

Cut the support blocks and attach them to the secondary frame, one at each corner. You may want to cut the blocks a bit on the fat side, then plane or sand them to fit. You want all eight "feet" on the ground.

4. Make the base socket. First, cut the socket segments to the dimensions specified by the "Cutting List." As you do this, rip converging bevels on the edges, as shown in the *Base Socket Detail*. Cut these bevels at 22½ degrees. (These segments are the same as the sliding collar segments but for their length.)

As you did in making the sliding collar, lay out the segments on two pieces of duct or packing tape. Roll up the segments to check how tight the seams will be and to see if the pole will fit into it okay. Make any adjustments necessary, either by planing material from mating surfaces, or by cutting new segments. When the parts are right, apply glue to the mating surfaces, roll the segments into the socket, seal the tape, and apply a band clamp.

Lay out and cut the socket's fingers next. Start on the socket's bottom end, scribing lines as shown in the *Base Socket Detail*. First scribe "diameter" lines to divide the area into quarters. Measure $15/16$ inch to each side of these two lines and scribe four more lines. These four lines will outline four triangular areas at the edges of the

BASE SOCKET DETAIL

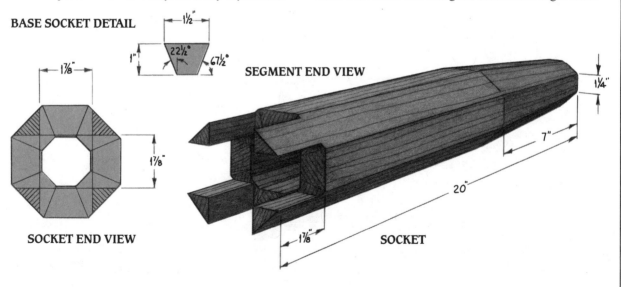

SEGMENT END VIEW

SOCKET END VIEW

SOCKET

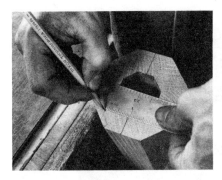

Here's how to lay out the cuts that create the four fingers that "clutch" the base assembly.

Left: With the socket blank in a vise, twice scribe its diameter, dividing the end into quarters (in the photo, the ruler covers the second line). *Center:* Measure and scribe a second set of lines—four in all—which are ¹⁵⁄₁₆ inch to each side of the first two lines. *Right:* The photo shows—among other things—the areas delineated by the layout lines. The fingers are the triangular areas NOT X'ed. Every segment that has an X is to be cut away.

With the fingers delineated on the end of the socket, extend lines onto the socket sides. With the tongue of a small steel square butted against the end of the socket, scribe along the inner edge of the body (or blade). Measure and mark how deep to cut along the line.

socket. These are the fingers. To complete the layout, extend lines from the corners of these triangles 1⅞ inches up the sides of the socket, thus establishing the length of the fingers. Connect these lines around the perimeter of the socket. To avoid confusion as you cut at the band saw, outline the four triangular areas that are the ends of the fingers, and mark the waste—Fred used Xs.

Before actually cutting, double-check your layout against the actual dimensions of the crosspieces to assure a snug fit. Cut out the waste on the band saw. To ensure a snug fit, cut shy of your layout lines. Check the fit, and trim on the band saw or pare with a chisel, as appropriate.

Clamp the nearly completed socket in a vise and taper the top end with a hand plane. The taper should start just above the point where the diagonal braces will be mortised in. (See the *Stand Side View.*)

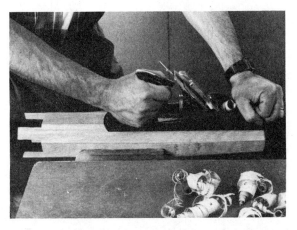

Hand plane the socket to get the taper. Clamp the socket in a vise and work with a jack plane. The degree of taper is an aesthetic judgment. The *Base Socket Detail* gives some indication of what we did, but you can alter the profile of the taper to suit yourself.

---

5. **Make the diagonal braces.** Cut the four diagonal braces to size, mitering the ends at 45 degrees in the process. The tenons are surprisingly easy to cut on the table saw. The miter gauge—set to the desired 45 degree angle—guides the workpiece and establishes the proper tenon angle. The distance from the (outside of the) blade to the fence is the length of the tenon. The first cut, made with the end of the workpiece butted against the fence, establishes the tenon shoulder. Repeated subsequent cuts remove the waste.

Set the depth of cut to properly establish the thickness of the tenon. After you've cut the tenon, redirect it by nipping off the corners, as shown in the *Brace Tenon Detail*.

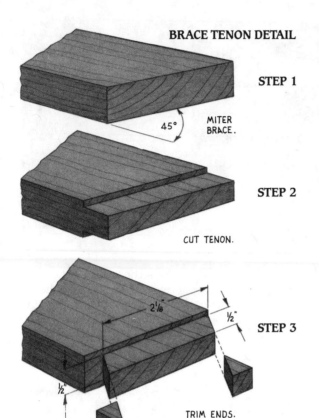

BRACE TENON DETAIL

STEP 1

45° MITER BRACE.

STEP 2

CUT TENON.

STEP 3

2⅛"

½"

½"

TRIM ENDS.

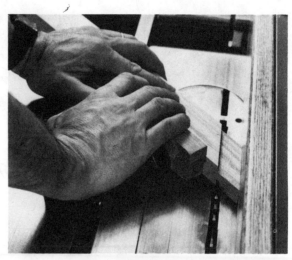

Cut the brace tenons on the table saw, using the fence and miter gauge to guide the work and control the cut. Here, one side has been cut, and the second side is just being started. Angling the miter gauge as shown helps hold the workpiece to the fence; if the gauge were angled the opposite way, the work would tend to drift away from the fence as you cut. The wood backing on the miter gauge—a common enhancement—offers better support for the workpiece.

6. **Cut the mortises for the diagonal braces.** Lay out the mortise locations on the crosspieces and the socket, as shown in the *Stand Side View*. To establish the starting point for measurements on the crosspieces, set the socket in place and scribe a line along the socket on each crosspiece. Measure from this line to the far end of the mortise, then measure back to establish the mortise length.

To cut the mortises, bore out most of the waste on the drill press (or with a portable drill and a 90-degree guide). Set the stop to make the mortise depth equal the tenon length plus about 1/16 inch (to provide a glue pocket). Drill a series of holes inside the mortise lines, using a bit equal to the mortise width. Then clean up the walls of the mortise with a chisel.

TIP

Getting the diagonal braces to fit their mortises precisely is pretty tricky because of the way the brace position shifts as the piece seats against the socket and crosspieces. You can circumvent fitting problems if you (a) wait to trim the tenons until after the mortises are cut, and (b) cut the mortises short. Fit the tenons to the socket mortises first. Then, with the braces fitted to the socket, lower it onto the crosspieces and mark the tenons for trimming.

7. **Assemble the entire base.** Dry assemble all the parts one last time to make sure everything fits. Radius the exposed edges of all parts with a router and a 1/4-inch rounding-over bit. To ensure that the rounded edges blend into one another where parts connect, mark these spots while the unit is still dry assembled.

To assemble the base, first glue the crosspieces together, then add the secondary frame. Glue the diagonal braces to the socket, then lower the brace/socket assembly onto the crosspiece assembly.

After the glue has dried, touch-up sand the assembly and apply an exterior-grade penetrating oil.

Dry assemble the base to confirm how the parts fit. Work in this sequence: Join the crosspieces and fit the secondary frame in place. With the braces seated in the mortises cut into the socket, settle the brace-socket unit into place atop the base assembly. The fingers will settle into the crotches of the crosspieces, and the tenons on the braces will drop into their mortises. A rubber mallet is a good persuader.

Umbrella Covering

The fabric cover is a relatively simply sewing project. (Unless, of course, you've never sewn before.) The cover is made up of eight triangular panels, two octagonal patches, and eight small pockets that fit over the ends of the arms. You must hem all the pieces, then sew them together. If you *do* sew, the most difficult part of this project is dealing with all the layers of cloth, and manipulating the cover as it reaches completion—it is 10 feet in diameter, after all.

---

1. Cut the parts from the fabric. The cover is composed of eight wedge-shaped panels and an octagonal pole patch. Eight small pockets, each of which fits over the end of an arm, are sewn between panels. These pockets keep the cover on the umbrella. Study the *Cover Plan;* cut eight panels, eight pockets, and two caps to the sizes shown.

---

2. Stitch up the arm pockets. Each of the eight 6-inch-square pieces of fabric is hemmed, folded, and sewn into a pocket that fits onto an arm of the umbrella.

Start by sewing a flat, simple hem along one edge, as shown in the *Pocket Sewing Sequence*. Fold the piece across the hem and fold in the two adjoining edges. Starting at the hemmed end, sew the folded edges of the pocket together. As you reach the unhemmed end, fold in the ends of the fabric, then finish the seam, turning the pocket as you sew to continue the seam across the end, closing the end. The hemmed end remains open.

The pockets that fit over the arms and hold the cover onto the umbrella framework are made from a single square of fabric. The cloth is folded in half and sewed along two edges to form the pocket. As you sew, fold the cut edges of the cloth in so they won't unravel. Here the end edges and corners are folded in as the stitching progresses along the folded-in sides.

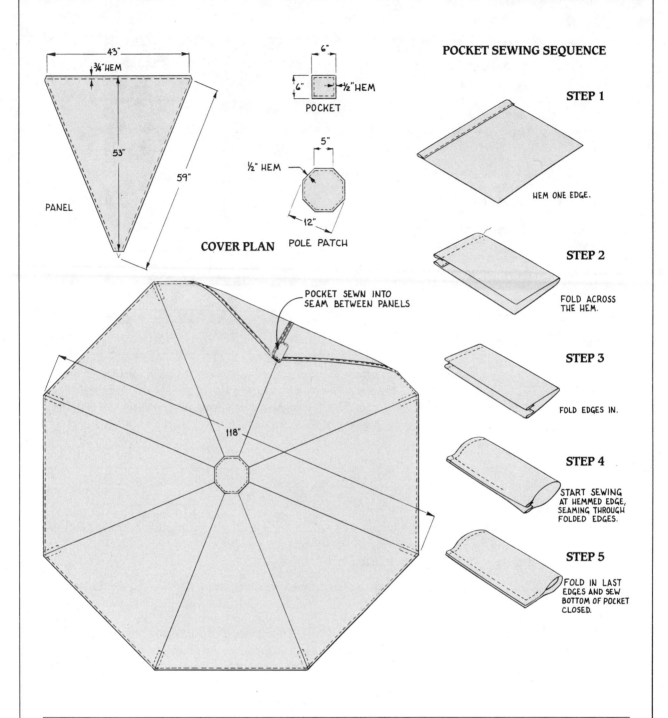

POCKET SEWING SEQUENCE

43"
¾" HEM
53"
59"
PANEL

6"
6"
½" HEM
POCKET

5"
½" HEM
12"
POLE PATCH

COVER PLAN

POCKET SEWN INTO
SEAM BETWEEN PANELS

118"

STEP 1
HEM ONE EDGE.

STEP 2
FOLD ACROSS
THE HEM.

STEP 3
FOLD EDGES IN.

STEP 4
START SEWING
AT HEMMED EDGE,
SEAMING THROUGH
FOLDED EDGES.

STEP 5
FOLD IN LAST
EDGES AND SEW
BOTTOM OF POCKET
CLOSED.

3. Hem and sew together the panels. Sew a double hem—the kind shown in the *Panel Hemming Sequence*—around the edges of each cover panel. As you do this, you'll discover the vexation of sewing "on the bias." Fabric has a grain, and it folds easily on the grain. But on the bias, which is crossing the grain, the cloth wants to unroll, making hemming pretty exasperating.

After the panels are hemmed, you must sew them together along their sides, sandwiching an arm pocket into each seam at the outer perimeter. To sew the panels, lay one on top of another, face to face. Line up the hemmed edges carefully, then stitch along the existing hem stitches, joining the two panels together. Start at the inside and sew toward the outer perimeter. When you get within 8 inches of the end, stop and tuck an arm pocket into the seam. The pocket's open end should face the cover's center, and the pocket itself should hang out of the seam like a tab. Line up the seam of the pocket with the panels' hems and sew. Work slowly because the needle must go through some 14 layers of fabric—eight layers in the hems of the pocket and six in the two panel hems. Finish the seam, sewing the pocket and two panels together.

Now unfold the panels and spread a third atop them, again face to face. Line up the hemmed edges and sew the third to the second. Again, as you near the outer perimeter, incorporate a pocket into the seam. In like manner, add the fourth panel and pocket, fifth, and so on, until the entire cover is sewn together.

Finally, bind the untidy ends of the panels along the pocket seam with a buttonhole or zig-zag stitch to reinforce and finish off the seam. Trim these ends with scissors.

PANEL HEMMING SEQUENCE

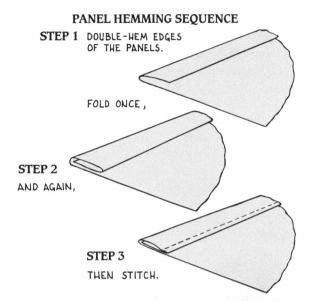

STEP 1 DOUBLE-HEM EDGES OF THE PANELS.

FOLD ONCE,

STEP 2 AND AGAIN,

STEP 3 THEN STITCH.

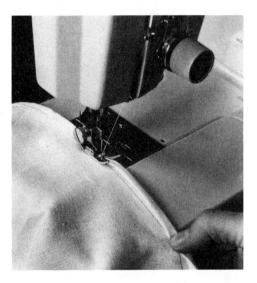

Above: Hemming the cover panels is as easy as this. With an ordinary #2 pencil, draw a line about ¾ inch from the cut edge. Fold the cloth once, then again, bringing the fold to the line. Sew along the centerline of the fold.

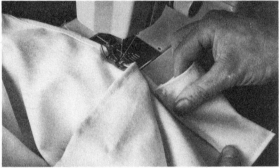

Top right: As you sew the panels together, tuck an arm pocket into the seam, just at the outer perimeter of the cover. The open end of the pocket faces the center of the umbrella, the hems all overlap, and the pocket is on the underside of the cover (with all the hems). *Center right:* When you are done, the seam will end in an untidy clump. *Bottom right:* Using a buttonhole stitch, reinforce the corner, then trim off the frayed edges and errant threads.

4. **Finish off the cover's center hole.** The center of the cover is an untidy opening—frayed seams and hems and stray threads. If you fit the cover on the umbrella frame now, the pole and the hardware connecting the arms to it will jut through the hole. A two-piece octagonal patch fits over (and under) this hole, providing a reinforced cover over the pole top and handsomely finishing off the cover.

Double-hem the two octagonal pieces of cloth already cut for the patch. Lay one patch atop the other, faces out, and carefully align the hems. Sew a circular seam, about 4 inches in diameter, in the center of the two patches, joining them together. Fit the patch into the hole, and arrange one layer of the patch overlapping the cover underneath and the other overlapping on top. Center and align the patch, and stitch around its edges, fastening it to the cover.

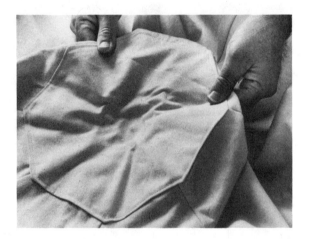

FITTING THE PATCH

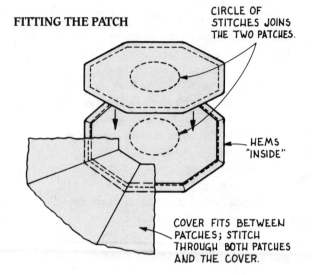

CIRCLE OF STITCHES JOINS THE TWO PATCHES.

HEMS "INSIDE"

COVER FITS BETWEEN PATCHES; STITCH THROUGH BOTH PATCHES AND THE COVER.

This last operation is easier said than done. Starting at the outer perimeter of the nearly 10-foot-diameter cover, you have to carefully work it under the foot of the sewing machine until the central area is beneath the needle. As you pull the cover under the foot, roll it up to make it a bit easier to maneuver through the sewing machine.

When the cover is all done, the top looks like this. The loose ends of the panels are concealed by the octagonal center patch. The patch's corners are aligned with the seams between panels, and the whole is neatly stitched together.

5. **Fit the covering onto the frame.** With the umbrella pole clamped upright either in a vise or in the base, open it about halfway. Drape the covering over the open frame, and slip the pockets over the ends of the arms, starting with one arm and working around the circumference of the frame.

After you've installed the cover, push up on the collar to open the umbrella more fully and to stretch the cover tight.

MAHOGANY ENSEMBLE

Exotica Made from Commonplace Flooring

Challenged to come up with a different sort of chaise lounge, our woodworkers turned to 5/4 mahogany and the saber saw.

MAHOGANY ENSEMBLE CHAISE LOUNGE

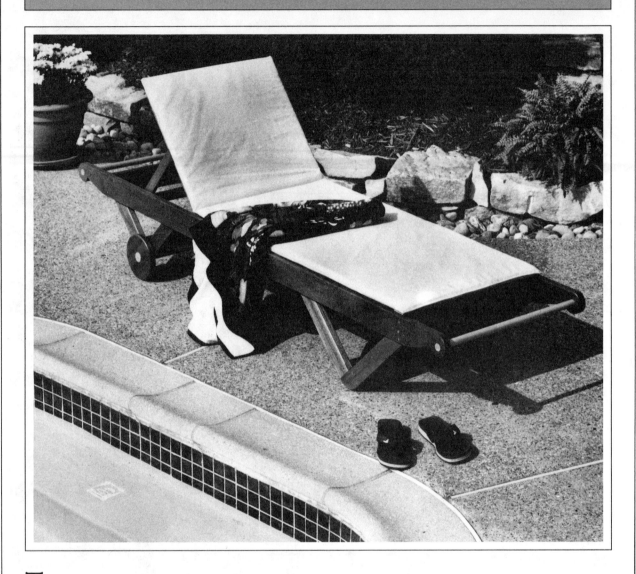

The genesis of this entire ensemble is this chaise lounge. An attractive, lean—but strong—wooden chaise lounge isn't easy to find. You certainly can't buy one for less than a king's ransom. And plans usually involve a load of 2 × 4s spiked together into a crate-like affair.

Thus challenged to come up with something a little different, Rodale woodworkers Fred Matlack and Phil Gehret turned to 5/4 (five-quarter) mahogany for their basic material and to the saber saw to execute a few embellishments.

The result is a chaise lounge that is interesting and relatively inexpensive to build, yet has great weatherability, good strength, and a lean, graceful appearance.

Too, the result was so inspiring that Fred 'n' Phil were sent back into the shop to create a folding serving cart, plans for which follow. That led to a plant cart project, and then to the chair and settee that round out the line.

All share the somewhat exotic material, the dowel-handle-in-scrolled-frame-end motif, the half-lap joinery.

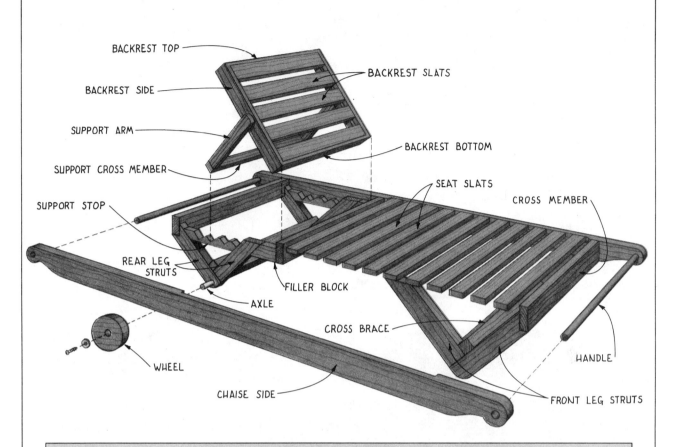

BACKREST TOP

BACKREST SIDE

SUPPORT ARM

SUPPORT CROSS MEMBER

SUPPORT STOP

REAR LEG STRUTS

AXLE

WHEEL

CHAISE SIDE

BACKREST SLATS

BACKREST BOTTOM

SEAT SLATS

CROSS MEMBER

FILLER BLOCK

CROSS BRACE

HANDLE

FRONT LEG STRUTS

CUTTING LIST

PIECE	NUMBER	THICKNESS	WIDTH	LENGTH	MATERIAL
Chaise sides	2	1¹⁄₁₆″	3½″	89″	5/4 mahogany
Cross members	3	1¹⁄₁₆″	3½″	22¾″	5/4 mahogany
Handles	2	1″ dia.		24⅛″	Hardwood dowel
Rear leg struts	2	1¹⁄₁₆″	2½″	14⅛″	5/4 mahogany
Rear leg struts	2	1¹⁄₁₆″	2½″	17″	5/4 mahogany
Front leg struts	2	1¹⁄₁₆″	2½″	17¾″	5/4 mahogany
Front leg struts	2	1¹⁄₁₆″	2½″	20¼″	5/4 mahogany
Cross braces	2	1¹⁄₁₆″	3⁹⁄₁₆″	22″	5/4 mahogany
Cross braces	2	1¹⁄₁₆″	2½″	19⅞″	5/4 mahogany
Seat slats	11	¾″	2½″	22¾″	1 × 4 mahogany
Backrest sides	2	1¹⁄₁₆″	2½″	19¾″	5/4 mahogany
Backrest top/bottom	2	1¹⁄₁₆″	2½″	20″	5/4 mahogany
Backrest slats	5	¾″	2½″	18½″	1 × 4 mahogany
Support arms	2	¾″	1½″	13″	1 × 4 mahogany
Support cross member	1	¾″	1½″	21½″	1 × 4 mahogany
Support stops	2	1¹⁄₁₆″	1½″	13½″	5/4 mahogany
Filler blocks	2	1¹⁄₁₆″	2¾″	5⅝″	5/4 mahogany
Axle	1	1″ dia.		26½″	Hardwood dowel
Wheels	2	1¹⁄₁₆″	7″ dia.		5/4 mahogany

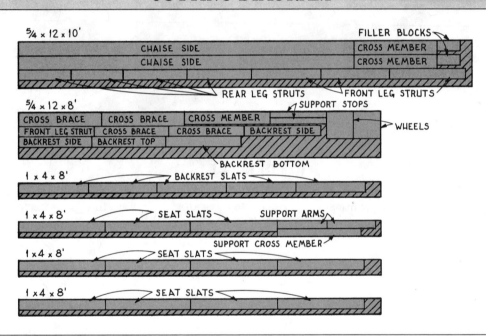

Builder's Notes

The chaise lounge is a good project for the woodworker with intermediate skills who is looking for a challenge. It doesn't require a shopful of tools to build—a table saw, a router, a saber saw, and a good drill are the major requirements. But the material takes you a step away from standard dimensional lumber without burdening you with the need to surface—or to pay someone else to surface—rough-sawn boards.

Materials. Mahogany is a relatively stable hardwood that, in our locale, anyway, is readily available in dimensional lumber form. That is, several lumberyards

normally stock mahogany in nominal 1-inch thickness and nominal 4-, 6-, 8-, 10-, and 12-inch widths, as well as nominal 5/4-inch thick stair tread. Stair tread is nominally 12 inches wide (an actual 11¼ inches); one edge is rounded over (or "nosed"), thus diminishing the stock's useful width.

The qualifier "normally" applies because we didn't always find the particular material we wanted in stock at the time we wanted it. When we built the ensemble's planter cart and chair and settee, the situation was normal. But months earlier, when we built this chaise lounge and the folding serving cart, our local yards had 1-by mahogany only in the form of tongue-and-groove 1 × 4.

Mahogany, at any rate, is an unusual wood, but it's one that fits into the everyday lumberyard vernacular with which every woodworker is familiar. For the woodworker hesitant to tackle hardwoods because they are stocked unsurfaced and in unpredictable dimensions, this is good to know. Of course, some woodworkers may have qualms about using a tropical wood like mahogany. For this project, there are the usual outdoor-wood alternatives—redwood, cedar, cypress. Or you could try using oak, maple, or some other hardwood available in your area.

In this project, both 1-by and 5/4 stock are used. We felt the basic chaise frame needed extra girth, but we didn't want the bulk of 2-by stock. So we turned to the 5/4 thickness—it usually dresses out to an actual thickness of 1 1/16 inch.

An unusual bit of hardware—the roto hinge—is critical to two of the projects in this ensemble, including the chaise lounge. A roto hinge consists of two hardwood discs that sandwich a metal washer slightly larger in diameter than the discs. The assembly is riveted together, with the rivet acting as a spindle. The wood allows the hinge to be glued in place, completely concealed from view.

If you can't locate roto hinges in your locale, you will find them available through many mail-order woodworking suppliers. It is a good idea to have the hinge in hand before drilling holes for it.

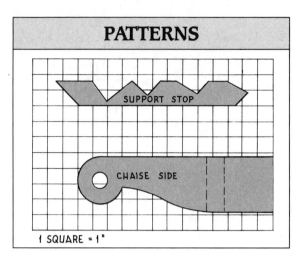

PATTERNS

SUPPORT STOP

CHAISE SIDE

1 SQUARE = 1"

Tools and techniques. This project is proof that you *can* do some out-of-the-ordinary projects without having a professional-level shop. A modest table saw, a basic-model router, a saber saw, and an electric drill are the principle tools required to build the lounger.

The saber saw comes into play to cut the scroll-like profiles on the ends of the sides. It also is used to cut odd-shaped notches in the leg struts and the support stops.

The router can be put to good use on this project: cutting the key dadoes, cutting the half-laps, rabbeting, rounding-over the edges of the piece. If equipped with a trammel attachment, the router can even be used to cut out the wheels. The step-by-step directions that follow include tips on jigs you can make to facilitate these router operations.

Finish. The finish we chose for all the projects in this ensemble is marine (or exterior) spar varnish. Made from tung and linseed oils or tung oil and phenolic resins, marine spar varnishes are *the* traditional clear outdoor finishes. In fact, for many years, they were the *only* clear outdoor finish.

What you need most of when applying marine spar varnish is patience. You want the oils to penetrate as deep as possible into the wood; to allow this, the varnish manufacturers add solvents to the mix that slow drying. So you must allow 6 to 24 hours between coats. Moreover, the manufacturers generally insist that many thin coats are better than a couple of thick coats. Three coats is just a minimum, six coats is preferable. Oh, and sand lightly between coats.

To prolong the finish, sand the piece and apply a fresh coat of varnish every year. Avoid leaving the furniture in the weather year-round, and minimize its exposure to direct sunlight.

Sewing. This project is a bit unusual in that we've included a cushion-making step, which involves not

TOOL LIST

Bar clamps	Ruler
Clamps	Saber saw
Drill	Sander(s)
1" dia. bit	Sandpaper
1" Forstner bit	Saw for crosscutting
Countersink bit	Screwdriver
Pilot hole bit	Sewing machine
Plug cutter	Table saw
Hand screw	Tack cloth
Paintbrush	Tape measure
Router	Trammel
3/8" rabbeting bit, piloted	Try square
1/4" rounding-over bit	Yardstick
3/4" straight bit	

PLAN VIEWS

1⅟₁₆"

22"

1⅟₁₆"

7" DIA.

1⅟₁₆"

TOP VIEW

RABBET FOR SLATS
⅜" WIDE x ¾" DEEP

SIDE VIEW

10"

1½" TYP.

2½" TYP.

1" DIA.

45°

45°

45°

45°

3½"

14"

7" DIA.

8½"

24"

48"

8½"

89"

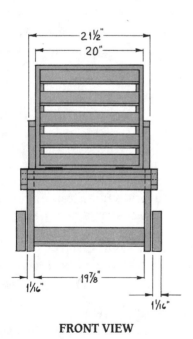

21½"

20"

19⅞"

1⅟₁₆"

1⅟₁₆"

FRONT VIEW

woodworking but sewing. If you are like me, you see sewing as an endeavor that *looks* pretty easy but is intimidating nonetheless. Without having actually done this sewing, I feel confident I could, especially with a little coaching.

The basic tool needed is a sewing machine, a standard, nothing-fancy sewing machine. You also need good scissors, some straight pins, maybe a few other oddments that anyone who sews will have. Depend on your coach.

The fabric we used is a natural-colored, 100 percent cotton sailcloth. It looks good in the photos, but it will get dirty quickly. Go to a fabric store and examine the goods. Sailcloth, you'll find, is a weight of cotton fabric that's between duck and canvas. You can use awning canvas, upholstery fabric, or any other sturdy fabric. While you are there, get thread to match the fabric you choose, and a slab or two of foam rubber.

Then follow the instructions. Still put off? Solicit help from someone who sews. Or hire the job out. Or just *buy* cushions.

1. Cut the chaise sides. Cut the sides to length from the 5/4 stock. Enlarge the chaise side pattern for the scrolled profile and the handle hole, and sketch it on both ends of each side. Cut the profile with a saber saw. Drill the 1-inch-diameter handle hole. To prevent the wood from splintering when the bit emerges, clamp a scrap back-up block to the workpiece.

With a router and a straight bit, cut three 1 1/16-inch wide, 3/8-inch deep dadoes to accept the cross members. Note the positions of the dadoes on the *Chaise Side Layout*. Because the largest commonly available straight bit is 3/4 inch, the trick here is to cut the dadoes to just the right width. A shop-made jig makes it easy to do.

Complete the joinery cuts on the sides by routing a

CHAISE SIDE LAYOUT

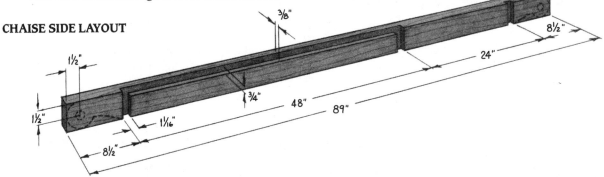

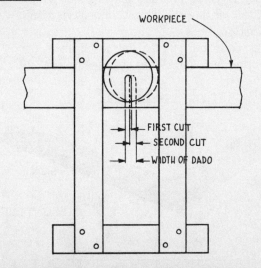

TIP

Since each chaise side has three wide dadoes, it is worth the trouble to make a modest router jig to help you cut them. To make the jig, you need two scraps of 1 × 4 stock about a foot long and two about 2 feet long. Fasten one guide strip (a long piece) to the two crossbars (the short pieces), making sure that the guide is exactly perpendicular to the crossbars.

Now calculate how far the second guide must be from the first to yield a dado that is 1 1/16 inches wide when using a 3/4-inch straight bit. Subtract the bit diameter from the base diameter, then add the width of the dado. Attach the second guide to the jig's crossbars, and cut a test dado on a scrap. If the dado is the correct width, your jig is ready to use on the side pieces. If the dado is too wide or too narrow, reposition the second guide.

To cut the dadoes, lay the jig on the side piece, as shown. Clamp the jig to both the workpiece and the workbench—we used a bar clamp for the former, a large hand screw for the latter. If you make your jig as large as we did, use an extra length of the working stock to support the overhang. In use, the two guide bars prevent the dado from inadvertently being cut too wide.

⅜-inch-wide, ¾-inch-deep rabbet along the top edge for the slats. The rabbet should extend from the front dado to the middle dado. Use a piloted rabbeting bit.

The final operation is to radius the inside edges of the handle cutouts, using a router and a ¼-inch rounding-over bit. The rest of the frame will be done after it is assembled, but the area around the handles will be difficult to reach with the router then.

2. Cut the cross members and handles, and assemble the frame. The cross members are cut from the 5/4 stock, the handles from 1-inch-diameter dowel.

After dry assembling the chaise frame to check the fits of the joints, apply glue and assemble the frame. Drive two or three 2-inch screws through the side and into the cross member at each joint. If a fully finished appearance is desired, countersink the screw heads and cover them with wood plugs.

After the glue has cured, rout a ¼-inch radius on the frame's edges. Doing this after assembly helps produce neat corners. Don't radius the rabbeted edges, of course.

3. Build the legs. The front and rear leg assemblies are constructed in the same way, but are slightly different sizes. To make each V-shaped assembly, two leg struts are joined in a half-lap joint. One strut is notched to fit the cross member, while the other is mitered at 45 degrees.

After crosscutting the leg struts to rough size, that is, about an inch longer than that specified by the "Cutting List," cut a half-lap on one end of each.

Glue up the assemblies. After the glue cures, lay out the miters and notches on the strut ends, scribe the 2½-inch-radius curve at the joints, and make these cuts with a saber saw.

Lay out and drill the 1-inch-diameter axle holes through the rear legs (the smaller pair).

Finally, radius the edges of the assemblies with a router and a ¼-inch rounding-over bit.

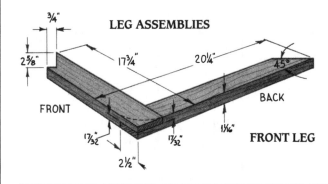

LEG ASSEMBLIES

FRONT LEG

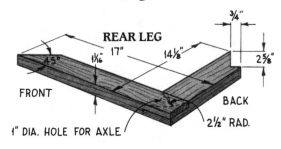

REAR LEG

4. Cut and assemble the cross braces. Each brace is constructed from two pieces of 5/4 stock. The longer of the two pieces is notched on each end, and the shorter is glued to it, forming a V-shaped brace that fits into the crooks of the leg assemblies and holds them apart.

Cut the pieces to length, then lay out and notch the longer pieces. You can cut one, then use it as a template to lay out the other. Glue the second part of each brace in place. Finally, radius the edges of the assemblies with a router and a ¼-inch rounding-over bit.

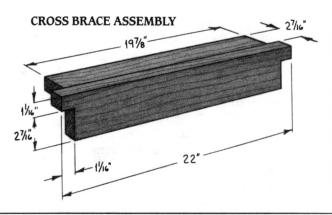

CROSS BRACE ASSEMBLY

TIP

You can cut half-laps on several struts at the same time using a router and a straight bit, so long as you cut them as cross-laps. Since with a router you trim only ¼ inch or so at a pass, you need to leave stock at the butt ends of the struts to support the tool. After the laps are cut, you trim the struts to their finished length, removing this excess stock.

Set up the work first. Line up several struts edge to edge, with scrap pieces on the outside. Align the butt ends and clamp them tightly together. Clamp a straightedge to the scrap pieces to guide the router and position the shoulder cut. To establish the length of the laps, cut a scrap to use as a spacer between the clamped-on straightedge and the router.

Chuck the appropriate bit in the router, set the depth of cut to about ¼ inch, and cut the shoulder of the laps (top photo). Fit the spacer in place and make the end cut, which should leave a bar of stock at the butt ends of the struts (center photo). Remove the spacer and rout the waste material from between the first two cuts (bottom photo). Reset the depth of cut and repeat the three steps until the laps are cut to the required depth.

Finally, unclamp the struts and trim them to length.

5. **Install the legs and cross braces.** Glue and screw the legs in place on the frame.

Fit the braces in place. Install them with glue and screws, countersinking the screw heads and covering them with wood plugs for a finished appearance.

6. **Cut and install the seat slats.** The slats are cut from 1-by stock. Radius the slat edges, then install the slats, spacing them evenly apart.

7. Build the backrest. The backrest consists of a 5/4 frame with slats that match the seat slats. It is hinged to the lounge and supported by a U-shaped support assembly that is attached to the back with roto hinges.

Cut the backrest parts from the 5/4 stock. Using a router and a rabbeting bit, machine a ⅜-inch-wide, ¾-inch-deep rabbet along one edge of each frame member, as shown in the *Backrest Assembly* drawing. Cut a 1 1⁄16-inch-wide, ⅜-inch-deep rabbet across the ends of the top and bottom frame members. Since the width of the rabbet exceeds the capacity of rabbeting bits, machine these rabbets the way you cut the half-laps.

Drill a stopped hole in each side member for a roto hinge. These must be positioned accurately so the support will pivot easily. For the chaise lounge, we used a roto hinge that penetrates ¼ inch into the wood and requires a 1-inch-diameter hole. Be sure you have the hinge in hand before drilling the hole, and make the diameter and depth to suit that hinge. A Forstner bit is best for this job, but a brad-point bit will work. The important thing is to make a clean, accurate hole that is deep enough to receive the hinge without having a center point go clear through the wood.

Assemble the back with glue and screws. Countersink the screw heads and cover them with wood plugs.

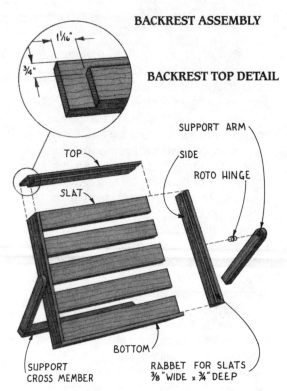

BACKREST ASSEMBLY

BACKREST TOP DETAIL

1 1⁄16"

¾"

SUPPORT ARM

TOP

SIDE

ROTO HINGE

SLAT

BOTTOM

SUPPORT CROSS MEMBER

RABBET FOR SLATS ⅜" WIDE x ¾" DEEP

Round-over the edges of the back. Don't round-over the rabbeted edge. Cut the slats and round-over their edges. Install the slats.

---

8. Build the support assembly. Cut the support arms and cross member. In the arms, drill 1-inch-diameter stopped holes for the roto hinges.

To properly radius the edges of the support assembly, you should assemble it with screws but no glue, rout the edges, then disassemble it.

Then mount the arms on the backrest with the roto hinges. Glue the hinge into the holes in the backrest, then apply glue and fit the arm over the hinge. Fasten the cross member in place with glue and screws.

---

9. Install the support stops. Enlarge the pattern for the support stops and sketch it on 5/4 stock. Cut two stops using a saber saw. They should fit snugly between the ends of leg struts. Screw them to the sides of the chaise.

Next, cut and install two filler blocks. The filler blocks fit between the middle cross member and the leg strut. They keep the back support from falling between the leg and the cross member if the back is pulled all the way forward. Screw the blocks to the chaise sides.

Finally, using two tight-pin hinges, install the backrest and the backrest support.

---

10. Make the wheels. The wheels are cut from 5/4 stock. They are 7 inches in diameter, with a 1-inch-diameter axle hole in the center. The wheels can be cut using a saber saw or a router; if you use a trammel accessory, you can do a better job of avoiding flat spots on your wheels.

11. **Finish the chaise.** Be sure all exposed edges are radiused. Sand all the surfaces, and wipe the resulting dust from the wood with a tack cloth.

Apply at least three coats of the spar varnish with a high-quality, fine-bristle varnish brush. Coat all the surfaces, including the underside of the chaise. Take particular care to coat any exposed end grain. Remember that with spar varnish, many thin coats add up to a better, more enduring finish than a couple of thick coats.

After the last coat of the finish is dry, install the axle and wheels. Slip the axle through the holes in the rear leg assembly. Fit a wheel over each end of the axle. Although you don't want to pinch the wheels, you don't need play in the assembly. Mark where the axle can be trimmed so it will be flush with the wheel on either side. Remove the wheels and the axle, and trim the axle. Before reinstalling the axle, locate the center of each end and drill a pilot hole for the screws that will secure the wheels.

With the holes drilled, reinstall the axle and wheels. Insert a screw through a fender washer and drive it into the pilot hole in the end of the axle.

12. **Make the cushions.** Cut a 76-inch piece of 45-inch-wide fabric for the cushion cover. The fabric's grain should parallel the larger dimension. Fold the piece once across the short dimension, with the back of the fabric exposed. Stitch a seam along the 76-inch dimension, ½-inch from the edge. Turn the resulting tube right-side out, so the fabric's face is now on the outside, and center the seam on the bottom.

Flatten the tube and sew two seams across it, as shown in *Sewing the Cushion,* 24 inches and 25½ inches from one end. These seams create two separate seat-cushion compartments. Turn in the fabric edges at both ends of the cover and hem them.

Cut the cushions from 1-inch-thick foam rubber. The seat is 21 inches by 48 inches; the back is 21 inches by 22 inches.

Stuff the foam cushions into the covers. Pin the ends of the covers shut with a row of straight pins at least 1 inch from the hemmed edge of the covers—you may have to temporarily bunch up the foam to get the pins in. This allows enough room to guide the layers of fabric under the foot of the sewing machine. Fold in the corners of the top and bottom layers of fabric approximately 1¼ inches. Sew a line of stitches through the hemmed edges of both layers of fabric, closing the ends of the covers. Remove the pins, allowing the cushion to unbunch. Place the cushions on the chaise.

SEWING THE CUSHION

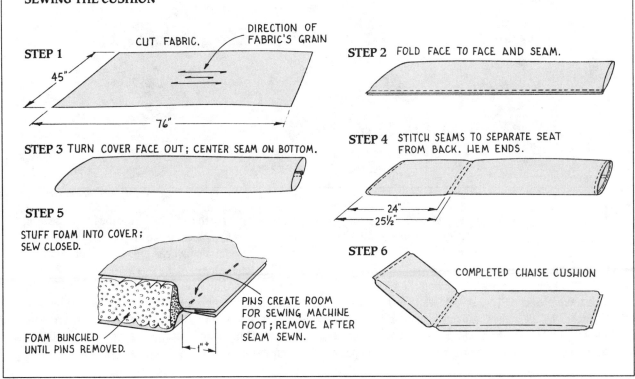

STEP 1 — CUT FABRIC. DIRECTION OF FABRIC'S GRAIN — 45" — 76"

STEP 2 FOLD FACE TO FACE AND SEAM.

STEP 3 TURN COVER FACE OUT; CENTER SEAM ON BOTTOM.

STEP 4 STITCH SEAMS TO SEPARATE SEAT FROM BACK. HEM ENDS. — 24" — 25½"

STEP 5 STUFF FOAM INTO COVER; SEW CLOSED. FOAM BUNCHED UNTIL PINS REMOVED. PINS CREATE ROOM FOR SEWING MACHINE FOOT; REMOVE AFTER SEAM SEWN. 1"+

STEP 6 COMPLETED CHAISE CUSHION

MAHOGANY ENSEMBLE FOLDING SERVING CART

Outdoor living isn't complete without a little something to nibble on. Burgers. Hot dogs. Barbecue chicken. Potato or macaroni salad. Chips. Iced tea or lemonade. Uummmm. That's real livin'.

This folding cart makes serving the picnic just a little more pleasant. The top surface is just a bit over 16 inches by 24 inches, expansive enough for a substantial cargo of food and drink. Load it with picnic-stuffs in the kitchen, then wheel it out to the deck or patio and park it next to the grill. If you tile the top or use a big ceramic trivet to protect the wood, you can even use the cart as a base for a small gas grill or hibachi.

The top is hinged to the legs at the end you'll use to wheel the cart, so it won't collapse when you lift the handle opposite the wheels to move it. Moreover, because the legs are joined to each other and to the top with concealed hinges, the cart won't fall into a heap of parts when you attempt to fold it for storage.

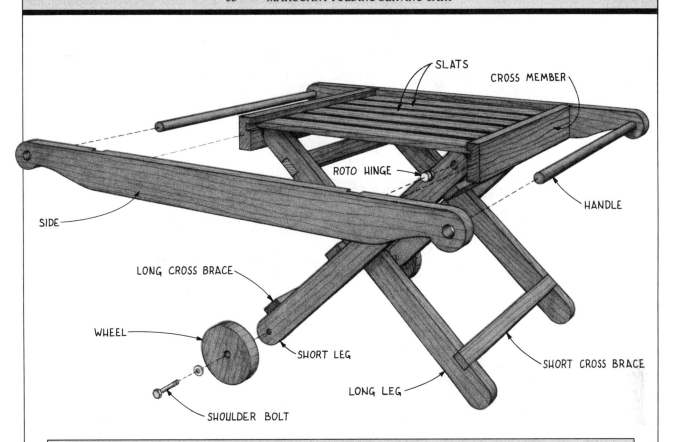

SHOPPING LIST

LUMBER

1 pc. 5/4 × 12 × 5' mahogany (stair tread)
1 pc. 1" dia. × 48" hardwood dowel
3 pcs. 1 × 4 × 8' mahogany

HARDWARE AND SUPPLIES

2 pcs. ½" × 1⅞" shoulder bolts
2 pcs. ⅜" flat washers
2 pcs. ⅜" T-nuts

HARDWARE AND SUPPLIES—CONTINUED

20 pcs. #6 × 1⅝" brass flathead screws
4 pcs. ¼" × 1" roto hinges
Resorcinol glue

FINISH

Spar varnish

CUTTING LIST

PIECE	NUMBER	THICKNESS	WIDTH	LENGTH	MATERIAL
Sides	2	1¹⁄₁₆"	3½"	44"	5/4 mahogany
Cross members	2	1¹⁄₁₆"	3½"	17⅛"	5/4 mahogany
Handles	2	1"		18½"	Hardwood dowel
Slats	6	¾"	2½"	25⅝"	1 × 4 mahogany
Long legs	2	¾"	1½"	38"	1 × 4 mahogany
Short legs	2	¾"	1½"	36"	1 × 4 mahogany
Long cross braces	3	¾"	1½"	16¼"	1 × 4 mahogany
Short cross braces	2	¾"	1½"	14¾"	1 × 4 mahogany
Wheels	2	1¹⁄₁₆"	7" dia.		5/4 mahogany

CUTTING DIAGRAM

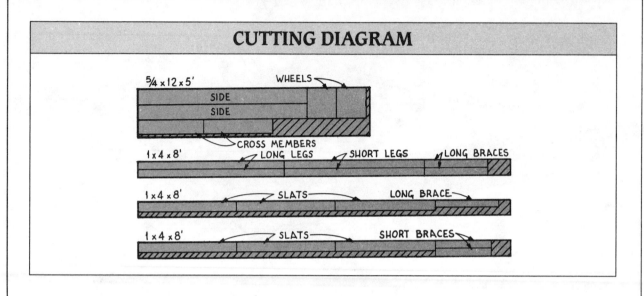

5/4 x 12 x 5'
SIDE
SIDE
WHEELS
CROSS MEMBERS

1 x 4 x 8'
LONG LEGS
SHORT LEGS
LONG BRACES

1 x 4 x 8'
SLATS
LONG BRACE

1 x 4 x 8'
SLATS
SHORT BRACES

PLAN VIEWS

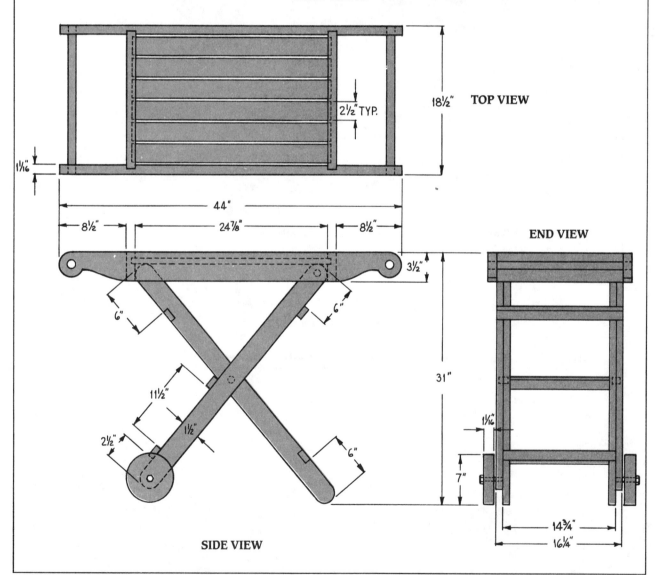

TOP VIEW

2½" TYP.

18½"

1¹⁄₁₆"

44"

8½"   24⅞"   8½"

3½"

6"   6"

11½"

1½"

2½"

6"

31"

END VIEW

1¹⁄₁₆"

7"

14¾"

16¼"

SIDE VIEW

PATTERN

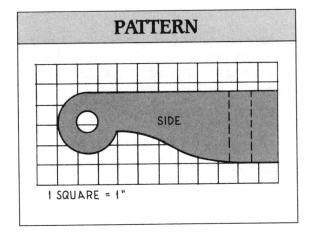

1 SQUARE = 1"

TOOL LIST

Bar clamps
Clamps
Compass
Drill
    ½" dia. bit
    1" dia. bit
    1" dia. Forstner bit
    Pilot hole bit
Paintbrush
Router
    ¼" rounding-over bit
    ¾" straight bit
    Edge guide

Ruler
Saber saw
Sander(s)
Sandpaper
Saw for crosscutting
Screwdriver
Table saw
Tack cloth
Tape measure
Trammel
Try square
Wrench

Builder's Notes

A companion project to this chapter's chaise lounge, plant cart, and settee and chair, the folding serving cart is constructed with the same materials and uses the same tools and techniques as those projects. If you are building only this project from the ensemble, then by all means read the "Builder's Notes" accompanying the chaise lounge project on page 54.

One hardware item, the shoulder bolt, is unique to the folding serving cart, but you should be able to get it at a well-stocked hardware store or home center. Sold as a replacement for a lawn-mower axle, a shoulder bolt usually has a ½-inch shank with ⅜-inch threads on the end. Because these bolts come in different lengths, you must match them to the wheels you make.

1. Cut the sides. Cut the sides to length from the 5/4 stock. Enlarge the side pattern for the scrolled profile and the handle hole, and sketch it on both ends of each side. Cut the profile with a saber saw. Drill the 1-inch-diameter hole. To prevent the wood from splintering when the bit emerges, clamp a scrap backup block to the workpiece.

With a router and a straight bit, cut two 1 1/16-inch-wide, ⅜-inch-deep dadoes to accept the cross members. Note the positions of the dadoes in the *Top Joinery* drawing. Because the largest commonly available straight bit is ¾ inch, the trick here is to cut the dadoes to just the right width.

Since you have four dadoes to cut, it is worth the trouble to make a modest router jig to help you with this operation. To make the jig (which is shown in the previous project), you need four scraps of 1 × 4, each about a foot long. Fasten one guide strip to the two crossbars, making sure that the guide is exactly perpendicular to the crossbars. The crossbars should snugly embrace the workpiece, so there is no play when the jig is fitted in place.

TOP JOINERY

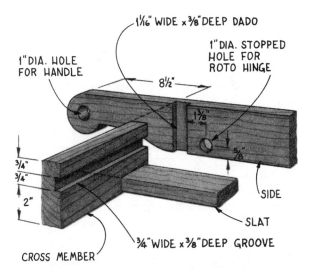

Now calculate how far the second guide must be from the first to yield a dado 1 1/16 inches wide when using a ¾-inch straight bit. From the diameter of the router base subtract the bit diameter and add the width of the dado. That's how far apart the two guides should be. *Clamp* the second guide to the jig's crossbars, and cut a test dado on a scrap. If the dado is the correct width, fasten the second guide in place, then cut the dadoes in the sides.

Next lay out and bore the stopped holes for the roto hinges that join the top assembly to the leg assembly. A Forstner bit is the best tool for the job, but a brad-point bit will work. The important thing is to make a clean, accurate hole that is deep enough to receive the hinge without having a center point go clear through the wood.

Note: Roto hinges are glued in place. Available in a variety of both depths and diameters, it's a good idea to get the hinges first, then drill the holes to fit. For this project, we'd recommend a fairly large size. The hinge should be inserted ½ inch into the wood and should require a hole ¾ to 1 inch in diameter.

The final operation is to machine a ¼-inch radius on the inside edges of the handle cutouts. The rest of the frame will be done after it is assembled, but the area around the handles will be impossible to reach with the router then.

2. Cut the cross members, handles, and slats. The cross members are cut from 5/4 stock, the handles from 1-inch-diameter dowel, and the slats from 1-by stock.

A ¾-inch-wide, ⅜-inch-deep groove must be plowed in each cross member to accept the slats, as shown in the *Top Joinery* drawing. This can be done using a table-saw–mounted dado cutter or a router equipped with an edge guide and fitted with a ¾-inch straight bit. If you rout the groove, be sure to make several passes, cutting deeper with each pass until the desired depth is achieved.

Using a router and a ¼-inch rounding-over bit, radius all the exposed edges of the slats.

3. Assemble the cart top. Dry assemble the top to check the fits of the joints. Check also to ensure that there's sufficient clearance between the top edges and the slats for your piloted rounding-over bit. You need to radius the edges of the top, and doing it after assembly helps produce neat corners. If it appears that the pilot will mar the slats, remove them, reclamp the top frame (without glue, of course), and machine the interior edges.

Proceed with the glue-up. Apply a spot of resorcinol glue to each slat, but don't spread any in the groove for the slats. The spot of glue should anchor the slat in position, yet still allow the wood to move with changes in humidity. One by one, insert the slats into the groove in one of the cross members. Use scraps of ¼-inch-thick stock as spacers to help you position the slats. After applying a dab of glue to the other end of each slat, work the second cross member onto them.

Now apply glue to the ends of the cross members and the dadoes in the sides. Fit the sides in place. Apply clamps across the assembly, one at each cross member.

After the glue has cured, use a router and a ¼-inch rounding-over bit to radius the frame's edges.

4. Cut the parts for the leg assemblies. Because one pair of legs has wheels, it is shorter than the other pair. And because the leg assembly without wheels fits inside the assembly with wheels, there are two different lengths of cross braces. As you cut the parts, label them lightly in pencil so you don't get them mixed up.

Lay out a 1¼-inch radius on both ends of each leg. Cut the radius with a saber saw or on a band saw. Sand the cut edges smooth, then, using a router and a rounding-over bit, radius all the edges of the legs only.

Don't radius the sections of the short legs where the cross braces will attach; mark these areas on the legs before you rout.

Notch the two long legs to accept cross braces, as shown in the *Leg Assembly* drawing. The short legs do not have the cross brace let in.

Lay out and drill the stopped holes in the legs for the roto hinges. As noted before, the holes should have a flat bottom, and you should have the hinges in hand to ensure the holes are properly sized for them. Locate the holes carefully so that the geometry of the leg assembly will be correct. Moreover, be sure you drill the holes for the leg hinges in one face of the short legs, and the holes for the top hinges in the opposite face.

Finally, lay out and drill the holes in the short legs for the T-nuts that secure the shoulder bolt axles. The ⅜-inch T-nuts require ½-inch-diameter holes.

LEG ASSEMBLY

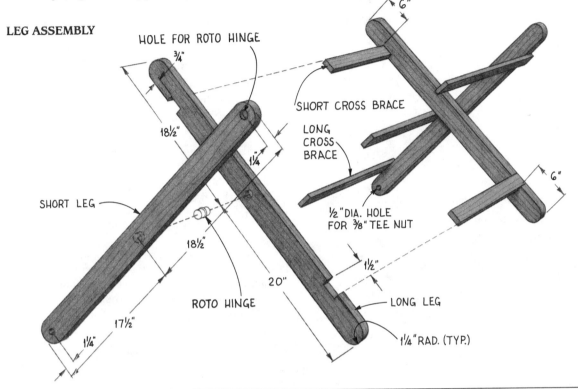

HOLE FOR ROTO HINGE

¾"

6"

SHORT CROSS BRACE

LONG CROSS BRACE

18½"

1¼"

SHORT LEG

½" DIA. HOLE FOR ⅜" TEE NUT

6"

18½"

ROTO HINGE

20"

1½"

17½"

LONG LEG

1¼"

1¼" RAD. (TYP.)

5. **Assemble the legs.** Dry assemble the two leg units separately. With a router and a rounding-over bit, radius the cross braces so their corners blend into the legs. It is easier to do this before the legs and top are finally assembled.

Join the long legs and the short cross braces first. Use glue and two screws per joint. We used brass screws and left them exposed. Be sure the roto hinge holes face out. Glue the hinges in place. Glue the hinges in place on the top assembly as well.

One at a time, glue the short legs to the hinges, both those in the leg assembly and in the top. This goes best if you have help to manipulate the leg assembly while you coax the second short leg into place. Glue and screw the remaining three cross braces in place, as shown in the *Leg Assembly* drawing.

Test the fit of the roto hinge before gluing it in place. The metal washer between the wooden elements ensures the legs will be far enough apart to work smoothly. Note the area on the upper leg where the edges aren't rounded-over; this is where the cross brace attaches.

6. **Make the wheels.** The wheels are cut from 5/4 stock. They are 7 inches in diameter, with a ½-inch-diameter axle hole in the center. The wheels can be cut using a saber saw or router; if you use a trammel accessory, you can do a better job of avoiding flat spots on your wheels. Radius the edges of the wheels with a ¼-inch rounding-over bit in a table-mounted router.

7. **Finish the cart.** Be sure all exposed edges are radiused. Sand all the surfaces, and wipe the resulting dust from the wood with a tack cloth.

Apply at least three coats of the spar varnish with a high-quality, fine-bristle varnish brush. Coat all the surfaces, including the underside of the cart. Take particular care to coat any exposed end grain. Remember that with spar varnish, many thin coats add up to a better, more enduring finish than a couple of thick coats.

When the finish is dry, install the wheels. Insert the T-nuts from the inside of the leg. Use a ⅜-inch flat washer on the shoulder bolt to "capture" the wheel, and tighten the shoulder bolt into the T-nut.

A shoulder bolt has a segment of smooth shank that's larger in diameter than its threaded segment. It's probably used to hold the wheels on your lawn mower. Hold a washer at the hole in the wheel, fit the bolt through, and turn it into the T-nut in the leg.

TIP

With a shop-made trammel for your router, you can cut perfectly round wheels quickly and easily. The trammel is cut from ¼-inch plywood. Remove the plastic base plate from your router and attach the trammel in its place.

To cut the wheels for the cart, roughly lay both out on the wood. Drill their center holes.

Now chuck a small-diameter straight bit in the router and set the depth of cut to about ¼ inch. Slip a machine screw through the appropriate pivot hole in the trammel and into the center hole of the first wheel. Holding the bit just above the wood, turn on the router. Plunge the bit into the wood and swing the tool around the pivot, cutting a circular groove. Shift to the second wheel and repeat the process. Turn the stock over and start cutting the wheels from the second side, cutting two circular grooves around the center holes.

Now increase the depth of cut to ½ inch. Make a second cut on both sides for each wheel. If necessary, increase the depth of cut yet again, and rout the disks free.

MAHOGANY ENSEMBLE PLANTER CART

Flowers, shrubs, and trees are some of the nicest things about the outdoors. When we settle into our outdoor furniture, we're enjoying the sun, the breeze, the fresh air, *and* the flowers, shrubs, and trees—all the foliage and greenery we don't usually have indoors.

But you don't always have wonderful plants *right there* where you relax. Maybe the deck is elevated, or the patio tied into a driveway. Planters are nice in such situations, so we built this planter cart.

Designed around two huge clay pots, this cart allows you to keep colorful plants close by, regardless of where you are—on the deck or porch, terrace or patio. The cart enables you to move the plants to their favored conditions—always in the sun, always in the shade, whatever they prefer. The cart is attractive enough to have indoors; when cold weather arrives, protect your plants by wheeling the planter cart inside.

The cart borrows many of the ensemble's design and construction motifs: the scrolled handle brackets, the half-laps, the wooden wheels. As with the other projects in the ensemble, many of the elements are simply screwed together.

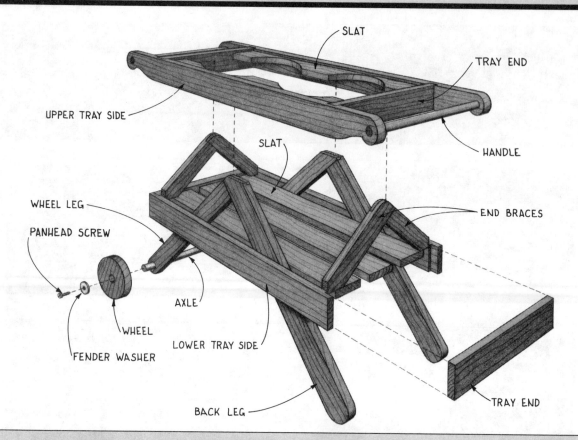

SLAT

TRAY END

UPPER TRAY SIDE

SLAT

HANDLE

WHEEL LEG

PANHEAD SCREW

END BRACES

AXLE

WHEEL

LOWER TRAY SIDE

FENDER WASHER

BACK LEG

TRAY END

SHOPPING LIST

LUMBER

2 pcs. 5/4 × 12 × 10' mahogany (stair tread)
3 pcs. 1" dia. × 36" hardwood dowel

HARDWARE AND SUPPLIES

1 box #6 × 2½" galvanized drywall-type screws
1 box #6 × 1¾" galvanized drywall-type screws

HARDWARE AND SUPPLIES—CONTINUED

2 pcs. #12 × 2" pan-head screws
2 pcs. 5/16" I.D. fender washers (minimum O.D. 1⅝")
Resorcinol glue

FINISH

Spar varnish

CUTTING LIST

PIECE	NUMBER	THICKNESS	WIDTH	LENGTH	MATERIAL
Upper tray sides	2	1"	3½"	52"	5/4 mahogany
Tray ends	4	1"	3½"	17¼"	5/4 mahogany
Lower tray sides	2	1"	3½"	38"	5/4 mahogany
Slats	5	1"	3½"	36"	5/4 mahogany
Wheel legs	2	1"	2½"	30½"	5/4 mahogany
Back legs	2	1"	2½"	31¾"	5/4 mahogany
End braces	4	1"	2½"	13"	5/4 mahogany
Wheels	2	1"	6"	6"	5/4 mahogany
Handles	2	1" dia.		18¾"	Hardwood dowel
Axle	1	1" dia.		19"	Hardwood dowel

CUTTING DIAGRAM

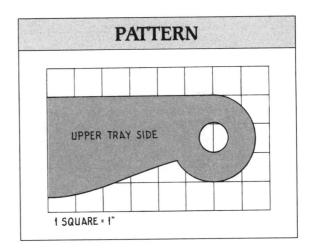

⁵/₄ × 12 × 10'

| LOWER TRAY SIDE | UPPER TRAY SIDE | TRAY END | WHEEL |
| LOWER TRAY SIDE | UPPER TRAY SIDE | TRAY END | |

BACK LEGS — END BRACES

⁵/₄ × 12 × 10' — WHEEL

| SLAT | SLAT | SLAT | |
| SLAT | SLAT | TRAY END | TRAY END |

WHEEL LEGS — END BRACES

Builder's Notes

A companion project to this chapter's chaise lounge, folding serving cart, and chair and settee, the planter cart is constructed with the same materials and uses the same tools and techniques as those projects. If you are building only this project from the ensemble, then by all means read the "Builder's Notes" accompanying the chaise lounge project on **page 54**.

The point worth noting is that wood doesn't always measure up to common standards. In this instance, the 5/4 (five-quarter) stock we purchased was a bit light of the common standard that 5/4 stock dresses out to—1 ¹/₁₆ inches. It was only 1 inch thick. The dimensions recorded here are based on what we used.

If your stock lives up to the standard, you shouldn't have to fret. Cut the dadoes and rabbets a tad wider, the

PATTERN

UPPER TRAY SIDE

1 SQUARE = 1"

laps a hint deeper. The extra thickness should have no other impact on your work.

---

1. Cut the parts for the upper tray. The cart is composed of two tray-like structures connected by the legs and two end braces. Start the project by making the upper tray, which has the scrolled ends and the handles.

Cut the sides, ends, and slats from the 5/4 stock and the handles from the dowel stock. Dado the sides for the ends, as shown in the *Upper Tray Joinery* drawing. Check the thickness of the stock, and cut the dadoes to the appropriate width. Use a router and a straight bit, and control the cut with the router jig described in the previous two projects in this chapter. The dadoes need only be ¼ inch deep.

To measure the pot, lay two scrap sticks against it. Shim them up so they clear the pot's rim. Measure between the sticks, adjusting their positions until they are both touching the pot and parallel. The distance between the sticks is the pot diameter.

PLAN VIEWS

TOP VIEW

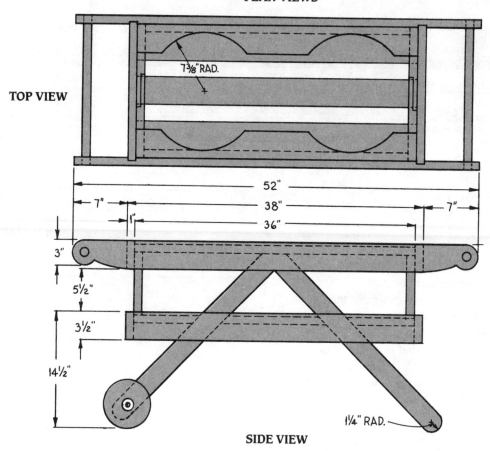

7⅜" RAD.

52"

7"   38"   7"

1"

36"

3"

5½"

3½"

14½"

1¼" RAD.

SIDE VIEW

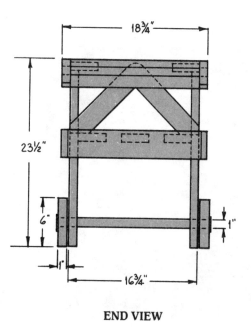

18¾"

23½"

6"

1"

1"

16¾"

END VIEW

TOOL LIST

Clamps

Combination square

Drill

  ⅜" plug cutter

  1" dia. bit

  Countersink bit

  Pilot hole bit

Paintbrush

Router

  ¼" rounding-over bit

  ¾" straight bit

Router, table-mounted

Ruler

Saber saw

Sander(s)

Sandpaper

Saw for crosscutting

Screwdriver

Table saw

  Dado cutter

Tack cloth

Tape measure

Trammel

Try square

Yardstick

Now enlarge the pattern for the scrolled ends, transfer it to the sides, and cut the shape with a saber saw or on the band saw. Sand the sawed edges to remove saw marks. Then bore a 1-inch-diameter hole through the center of the scroll.

Finally, cut two arcs in each slat, as shown in the

Top View. These arcs should be laid out to accommodate the specific pots you will use in the cart. The pots we used were a bit over 14 inches in diameter just beneath their rims. Measure your pots and adjust the radius of the arcs, if necessary. After cutting the arcs, sand the sawed edges to smooth them.

UPPER TRAY JOINERY

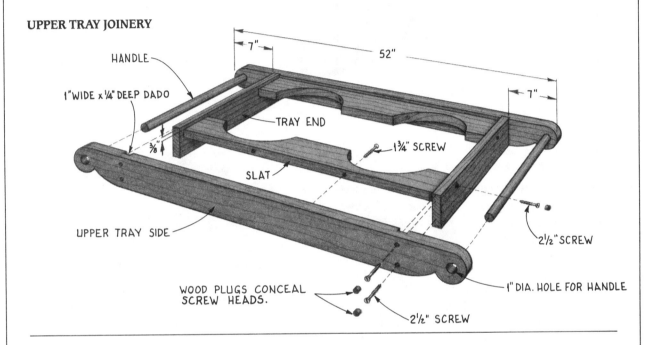

2. Assemble the upper tray. The initial step is to sand the parts and radius their edges. Use a router and a ¼-inch rounding-over bit to radius the edges that will be exposed. The interior corners of the framework should be left to be rounded during assembly so they can be blended for best appearance.

Assemble the sides and ends first. Be sure to incorporate the handles in the assembly at this time; it may be tough to drive them all the way through the holes after the frame is screwed together. Use resorcinol glue

and 2½-inch galvanized drywall-type screws. Countersink and counterbore the pilot holes for the screws so wood plugs can be used to conceal the screw heads. After the frame is assembled (but before the slats are attached), radius the inner perimeters—top and underside. That done, add the slats. Drive screws through the ends and sides into the slat edges, as well as through the edges of the slats (where the arcs reduce their width sufficiently) into the sides.

3. Make the lower tray. Cut the sides, ends, and slats for the lower tray. The ends fit into rabbets cut in the sides. Cut the rabbets as wide as the stock is thick and ¼ inch deep. Use a router and a straight bit guided by a straightedge clamped to the work.

Assemble the sides and ends temporarily with screws only, and radius the interior perimeter of the frame with the router and the rounding-over bit. This

done, back out the screws, disassembling the parts. Radius the remaining exposed edges of the sides, ends, and slats. Sand the parts.

Now glue and screw the slats between the ends. See the *Lower Tray Joinery* drawing. Be sure to counterbore all the pilot holes so the screw heads can be concealed beneath wood plugs. Don't attach the sides; they are attached after the tray is attached to the legs.

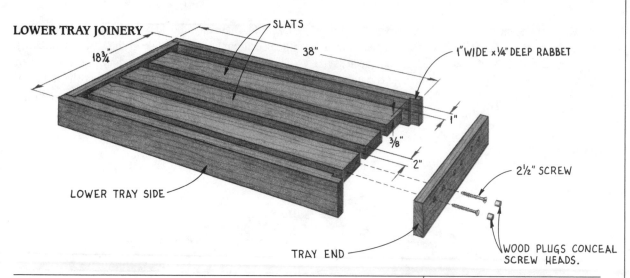

LOWER TRAY JOINERY

SLATS

18¾"

38"

1" WIDE x ¼" DEEP RABBET

1"

3/8"

2"

2½" SCREW

LOWER TRAY SIDE

TRAY END

WOOD PLUGS CONCEAL SCREW HEADS.

4. Make the leg and end brace assemblies.

Both the leg and end brace assemblies consist of two members joined in end laps, forming (when installed) inverted Vs.

Cut the parts to the sizes specified by the "Cutting List." Each piece has a lap cut on one end; do this next. Laps can be cut with several different tools: radial arm saw, table saw, or router. Since all members are the same thickness and width, one setup will serve for all. After cutting the laps, round off the foot ends of the legs; scribe a 1¼-inch radius on the leg, then cut it with a saber saw or on the band saw. Drill a 1-inch-diameter hole for the axle through the two wheel legs (the shorter legs); see the *Leg Assembly* drawing for the hole's location. Finally, trim the ends of the end braces, as shown in the *End Brace Assembly* drawing.

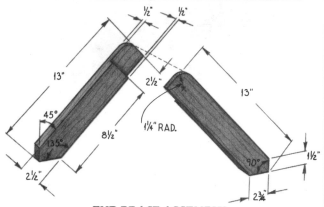

END BRACE ASSEMBLY

Glue up the assemblies with resorcinol glue. Be sure you mate a back leg and a wheel leg in each leg assembly. After the glue sets, trim the lap joints. The end braces are rounded slightly. The leg assemblies are trimmed on a 45 degree angle. Finally, radius the edges of these parts with a router and a ¼-inch rounding-over bit, and sand them carefully.

LEG ASSEMBLY

½"

2½"

31¾"

30½"

1"

135°

2½"

2½"

1¼" RAD. (TYP.)

TIP

Use a piece of the working stock as a measuring tool when setting the table saw fence for cutting laps. When you are joining two pieces of equal width in the lap joint, the length of the laps equals the width of the stock. Butt the stock against the fence, and adjust the fence to align the other edge of the stock with the *outside* of the blade.

5. Assemble the cart. Assembly of the cart is contrary; it progresses from the top down. The upper tray is already assembled. Turn it upside down on your workbench. On the bottom of the slats, mark the midpoint (one mark on each slat). Similarly, mark the centerline (the line that splits the angle between the legs) on each leg assembly. Set a leg assembly in place and line up the centerline of the assembly with the centerline of the upper tray. Align the legs and drive 1¾-inch screws through the legs into the back of the upper tray sides. While you should drill pilot holes for these screws, the holes don't need to be counterbored, since the screws aren't obviously visible.

Attach the lower tray next. Cut four spacer blocks of equal length—5½ inches. Stand the blocks on the edges of the upper tray and prop the lower tray—turned upside down, of course, and still without its sides—on them. To stabilize the legs while you drill pilot holes and drive screws, clamp them to the lower tray slats. Run a couple of 2½-inch screws through each leg into the slats; these screws will be concealed by the sides. Now attach the sides, driving 2½-inch screws into the previously drilled (and counterbored) pilot holes. Complete this assembly phase by driving a 1¾-inch screw through each leg into the back of the side; counterboring the pilot holes for these screws is optional.

It is important to align the leg assemblies correctly when attaching them to the top tray assembly. Use a speed square, a combination square, or—as here—a drafting triangle. With one screw driven, you can rock the assembly slightly until you have the proper 45 degree angle. Note the pencil mark indicating the centerline of the leg assembly; it is aligned with a similar mark indicating the center of the tray assembly.

Cut four 5½-inch-long scraps to rest the lower tray on during its installation. These silent helpers keep the trays parallel, and they eliminate the need for clamping and adjusting and reclamping. Be sure the tray is upside down. The leg assemblies are still unstable, so clamp them to the tray while you drill pilot holes and drive screws.

The lower sides go on after the legs are secured to the lower tray. They need to be attached first to the ends, then to the legs.

6. **Make the wheels.** The wheels are cut from 5/4 stock. They are 6 inches in diameter, with a 1-inch-diameter axle hole in the center. The wheels can be cut using a saber saw; if you use a trammel accessory for the saw, you can do a better job of avoiding flat spots on your wheels. Radius the edges of the wheels with a ¼-inch rounding-over bit in a table-mounted router.

Prepare the axle by drilling a pilot hole in the center of each end.

---

7. **Finish the cart.** All the exposed screws, primarily those driven through the faces of the sides and ends, should be covered with wood plugs. Make your own plugs from the mahogany scraps, using a plug cutter chucked in a drill. A ⅜-inch-diameter plug will probably be the correct size. Apply resorcinol glue to the counterbore with a cotton swab and press the plug into the hole. After the glue dries, pare the plug flush with the surface with a chisel.

Sand the plugs, and touch up any rough spots on the cart and its wheels. Be sure all exposed edges are radiused. Wipe any dust from the wood with a tack cloth.

Apply at least three coats of the spar varnish with a high-quality, fine-bristle varnish brush. Coat all the surfaces, including the underside of the cart. Take particular care to coat any exposed end grain. Remember that with spar varnish, many thin coats add up to a better, more enduring finish than a couple of thick coats.

After the last coat has dried, fit the axle in place and install the wheels. Fit a wheel over the axle stub protruding from the leg and secure it with a pan-head screw and fender washer.

Like the ideal donut, a fender washer is all washer and very little hole. But it's the perfect retainer for the wheel. Just make sure the washer is larger in diameter than the axle. Install the wheels after the finish has dried.

MAHOGANY ENSEMBLE CHAIR AND SETTEE

To round out the Mahogany Ensemble, we needed some seats. Here they are: a chair and a settee.

Made with the ensemble's signature motifs, the pieces have the scrolled post tops, the half-lap joinery, the 5/4 (five-quarter) mahogany construction. Like the chaise lounge, the chair and settee are cushioned with foam rubber mats covered with natural sailcloth. Although

somewhat too erect to allow for total relaxation, they are a big improvement over picnic benches for outdoor socializing.

One of the nicest things about the assembly concept is that you can adjust the height and rake of the seat during construction. I'm pretty tall and unnecessarily large; Phil Gehret, who built a lot of this furniture, is less

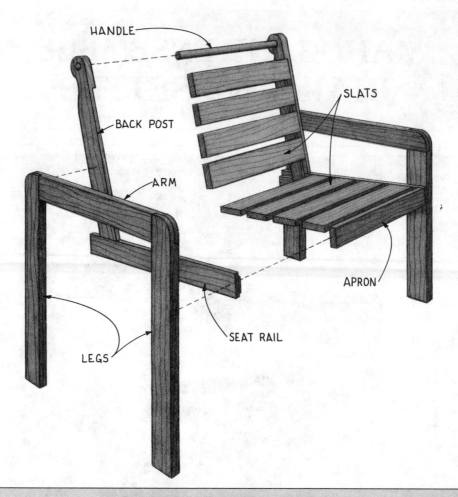

HANDLE

BACK POST

ARM

SLATS

APRON

SEAT RAIL

LEGS

SHOPPING LIST—CHAIR

LUMBER

2 pcs. 1 × 4 × 8' mahogany
1 pc. 5/4 × 12 × 6' mahogany (stair tread)
1 pc. 1" dia. × 36" hardwood dowel

HARDWARE AND SUPPLIES

1 box #6 × 1⅝" galvanized drywall-type screws
Resorcinol glue

FINISH

Spar varnish

FABRIC AND NOTIONS

1⅛ yd. 45" wide upholstery fabric
1 spool matching thread
1 pc. 1" × 16" × 21" foam rubber
1 pc. 1" × 18" × 21" foam rubber

SHOPPING LIST—SETTEE

LUMBER

4 pcs. 1 × 4 × 8' mahogany
1 pc. 5/4 × 12 × 8' mahogany (stair tread)
2 pcs. 1" dia. × 36" hardwood dowel

HARDWARE AND SUPPLIES

1 box #6 × 1⅝" galvanized drywall-type screws
Resorcinol glue

FINISH

Spar varnish

FABRIC AND NOTIONS

2¼ yd. 45" wide upholstery fabric
1 spool matching thread
1 pc. 1" × 16" × 41" foam rubber
1 pc. 1" × 18" × 41" foam rubber

CUTTING LIST—CHAIR

PIECE	NUMBER	THICKNESS	WIDTH	LENGTH	MATERIAL
Back posts	2	1"	2½"	24"	5/4 mahogany
Seat rails	2	1"	2½"	22"	5/4 mahogany
Apron	1	1"	2½"	20"	5/4 mahogany
Slats	8	¾"	3½"	20"	1 × 4 mahogany
Arms	2	1"	2½"	22"	5/4 mahogany
Legs	4	1"	2½"	24"	5/4 mahogany
Handle	1	1" dia.		21"	Hardwood dowel

CUTTING LIST—SETTEE

PIECE	NUMBER	THICKNESS	WIDTH	LENGTH	MATERIAL
Back posts	3	1"	2½"	24"	5/4 mahogany
Seat rails	2	1"	2½"	22"	5/4 mahogany
Center support rail	1	1"	1¾"	21¼"	5/4 mahogany
Apron	1	1"	2½"	40"	5/4 mahogany
Slats	8	¾"	3½"	40"	1 × 4 mahogany
Arms	2	1"	2½"	22"	5/4 mahogany
Legs	4	1"	2½"	24"	5/4 mahogany
Handle	1	1" dia.		41"*	Hardwood dowel

*Use 2 dowels, joined at the center support.

tall and more svelte. Chairs he built to accommodate himself don't comfortably accommodate me. But this design has the solution: As you'll see, you can clamp the parts together, give 'em a sit, and make some adjustments before final assembly. So I can raise the seat and tip it back just to accommodate *me*. It's nice.

Another plus is the cushion design. As covered, the seat and back cushions are a single unit. The cover is a simple fabric tube with a foam rubber slab stuffed into each end. A double seam stitched across the middle separates the seat from the back, but leaves them linked. The covers are simple enough to sew that even a woodworker can do it.

Builder's Notes

A companion project to this chapter's chaise lounge, folding serving cart, and planter cart, the chair and settee are constructed with the same materials and use

PATTERN

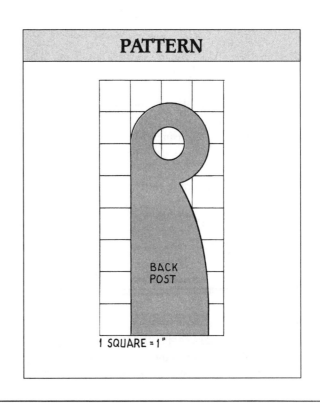

BACK POST

1 SQUARE = 1"

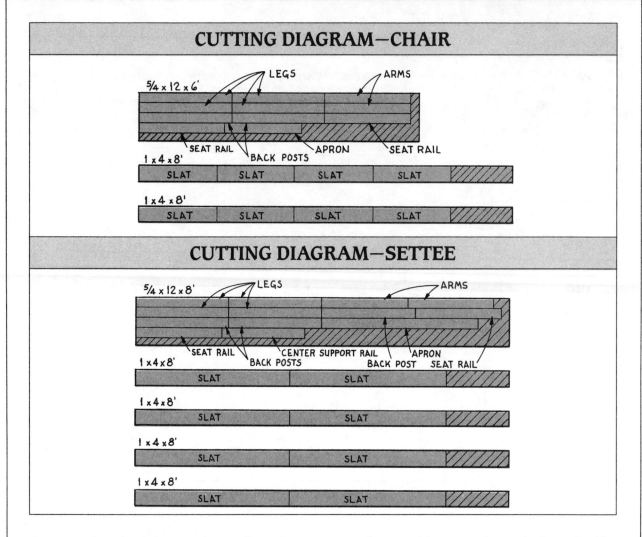

CUTTING DIAGRAM—CHAIR

CUTTING DIAGRAM—SETTEE

the same tools and techniques as those earlier projects. If you are building only this project from the ensemble, then by all means read the "Builder's Notes" accompanying the chaise lounge project on page 54.

The point worth noting with this project is that wood doesn't always measure up to common standards. In this instance, the 5/4 stock we purchased was a bit light of the 1 1/16-inch standard that 5/4 stock usually dresses out to. It was only 1 inch thick. The dimensions recorded here are based on what we used.

If your stock lives up to the standard, you shouldn't have to fret. Cut the laps a hint deeper. The extra thickness should have no other impact on your work.

As is the case with many of the outdoor seats in this book, the chair and settee differ only in the length of the members that connect the side frames—in this case, the handle, slats, and apron. To bolster the structure, a center support rail is added midway between the side frames of the settee.

1. Cut and lap the arms and legs. Both the chair and the settee consist of two side frames, each made up of an arm and a pair of legs, and a seat assembly. Make the side frames first. To that end, cut the arms and legs to the sizes specified by the "Cutting List."

Cut the laps that join the legs and arm into a side frame. The legs are lapped on one end, the arms on both

ends. These are easily cut on a radial arm or table saw using a dado cutter. On the table saw, guide the workpiece with the miter gauge and set the rip fence to govern the length of the lap. On the radial arm saw, clamp a stop to the backstop to govern the lap's length. Either way, you'll have to make three or four passes to complete each lap.

TIP

To set the depth of cut for a half-lap, make trial cuts on scraps of the working stock. This approach works whether you use a radial arm saw or table saw, and a standard blade or a dado cutter.

Set the depth of cut roughly, using a rule. Then set the miter gauge (or the arm) to a slight angle. Nip a corner of a piece of scrap. Roll the piece over and nip the opposite corner, so the two cuts intersect. By looking at the end of the piece where the cuts intersect, you'll be able to tell how you need to adjust the depth of cut. Adjust the setting, then try it on the new scrap.

In the photo, the scraps show settings that are (from left to right): just right, too deep, and too shallow.

2. Assemble the side frames. With resorcinol glue, assemble the side frames. Clamping each joint with a hand screw eliminates struggling with cauls needed to protect the woodwork from the metal pads or jaws of other sorts of clamps. But if C-clamps or speed clamps are what you have, they are more than adequate.

After the glue has set, scribe a 2½-inch radius on each lap joint, as shown in the *Side Frame Joinery* drawing, and round off the corners with a saber saw or on the band saw. Then radius the edges of these assemblies with a router and a ¼-inch rounding-over bit.

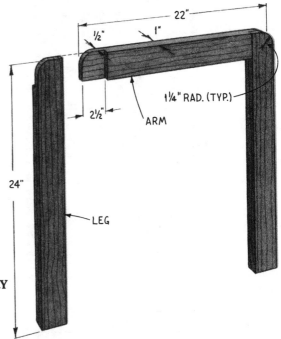

SIDE FRAME JOINERY

3. Cut the parts for the seat assembly. The seat assembly for the chair is composed of seat rails, back posts, slats, and an apron. The rails and posts are joined into two L-shaped frames by half-laps. In turn, the two frames are connected by the apron and slats, which nestle into rabbets cut in the rails and posts. The settee, besides having longer slats and apron, has a center support rail that's a trimmed-down seat frame.

Cut the necessary parts to the sizes specified by the "Cutting List."

Enlarge the pattern for the scrolled post top and transfer it to the posts. Cut the scroll with a saber saw or on the band saw. Bore the 1-inch-diameter hole for the handle.

CHAIR PLAN VIEWS

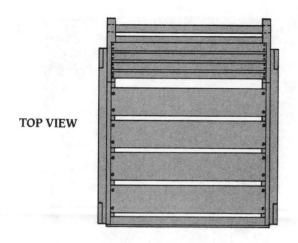

TOP VIEW

TOOL LIST

Clamps	Sandpaper
Compass	Saw for crosscutting
Drill	Sawhorses
1" dia. bit	Screwdriver
Pilot hole bit	Sewing machine
Paintbrush	Table saw
Router	Dado cutter
¼" rounding-over bit	Miter gauge
½" rabbeting bit	Tack cloth
Ruler	Tape measure
Saber saw	Try square
Sander(s)	

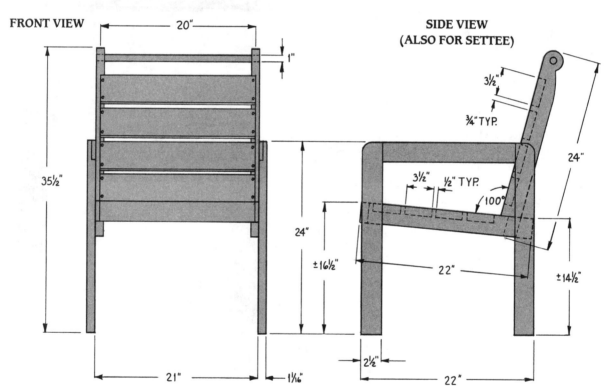

FRONT VIEW

SIDE VIEW (ALSO FOR SETTEE)

4. Cut the joinery in the rails and posts. Study the *Rail-to-Post Joinery* drawing next, so you understand what needs to be accomplished.

Rabbet the rails and posts first. As shown, the rabbets are ½ inch wide and ¾ inch deep. On the rails, the rabbet for the slats extends from one end to the other. A rabbet is also cut across one end for the apron. On the posts, the rabbet for the slats is stopped, extend-

ing 20½ inches from the bottom. Note the orientation of the rabbet to the scrolled post top. *All the rabbets are on the inside face of each piece;* when assembled, the seat frames are mirror images of each other.

The rabbets can be cut with a router or on the table saw with a dado cutter. However you cut the rabbets, square the stopped end of the rabbet in the post with a chisel.

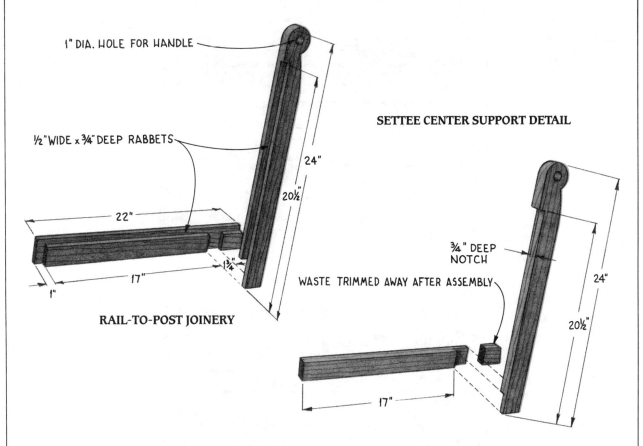

1" DIA. HOLE FOR HANDLE

½" WIDE x ¾" DEEP RABBETS

24"

20½"

22"

17"

1¾"

1"

RAIL-TO-POST JOINERY

SETTEE CENTER SUPPORT DETAIL

¾" DEEP NOTCH

WASTE TRIMMED AWAY AFTER ASSEMBLY

24"

20½"

17"

Cut the half-laps that join the rails and posts next. The laps on the posts are fairly straightforward, but those on the rails really make the case for the radial arm saw as the best tool for cutting laps. On this tool, you merely position the stop, set the arm's angle, and make the cuts.

The task is more complicated on the table saw. Begin the posts by mitering the lower ends; the miter, measured from the rabbeted edge to the butt end, must be 80 degrees. To actually cut the laps, set up the table saw with the dado cutter and position the rip fence as you did to cut the leg and arm laps. To cut the first lap, set the miter gauge to form a 100 degree angle with the fence. Pick the post that will lay in the miter gauge with its mitered end against the fence *and* the rabbet up. Cut the lap in it. Now readjust the miter gauge to form a 70 degree angle with the fence. Lap the other post.

The laps in the rails are harder to cut; you can't use the fence because the ends must be square rather than mitered, and the workpiece conceals the cut. So lay out the laps and extend the lines for the shoulder cuts onto the edges of the workpiece. Guiding the piece with the miter gauge, align the lines with the cutter and make the cuts. The laps in the rails are cut into the rabbeted face.

Note: The center support rail for the settee is

essentially a duplicate of a seat frame with the rabbet trimmed off. See the *Settee Center Support Detail*. The rail is specified by the "Cutting List" to be ¾ inch shorter and ¾ inch narrower than the seat rails. It is not rabbeted at all. The post is the same size as the other posts. Instead of rabbeting it, however, notch this post to the depth and length of the rabbets in the other posts. Cut laps in the center support parts just as in the seat frame parts.

TIP

If you choose to rout the rabbets in the posts and rails, you can use a ½-inch rabbeting bit and address the workpiece from its edge. To provide more surface area for the router to bear on, gang the two rails and two posts together and clamp them. Rout one rabbet. Shift the parts around to expose a new one, then rout the rabbet in it. And so forth. If you work this way, cut each rabbet in multiple passes, routing about ⅛ inch deeper with each pass.

SETTEE PLAN VIEWS

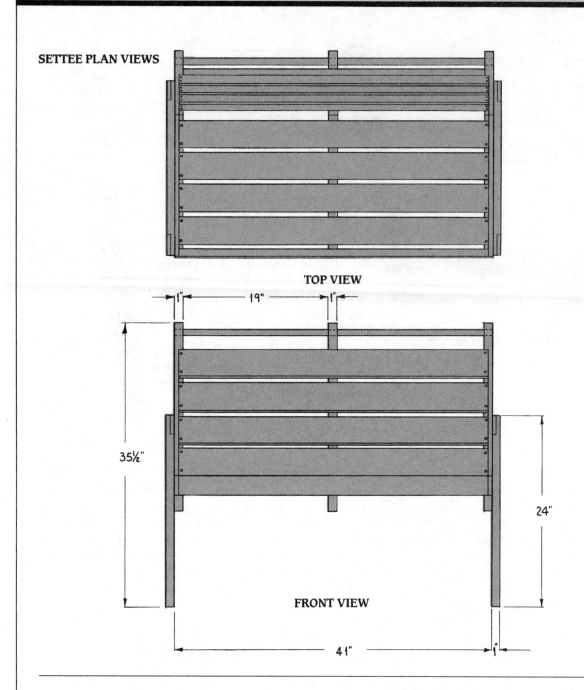

TOP VIEW

FRONT VIEW

35½"

19"

1"   1"

24"

41"

1"

5. Assemble the seat. Glue up the seat frames (and center support, if applicable) first, using resorcinol glue. After the glue has set, you can trim off the rear projection on the center support, since it serves no purpose. (On the seat frames, the projection is an attachment point for the side frames.) After the glue has dried and the clamps are off, radius all the exposed edges with a router and a ¼-inch rounding-over bit. Radius the edges of the slats and apron as well.

Attach the handle and the apron next, joining the two seat frames. Glue the handle into one seat frame, then add the other frame. (When making the settee, slide the center support onto the handle before adding the second seat frame.) With the frames linked by the handle, it's relatively easy to glue and clamp the apron in place.

After the glue has dried, install the slats. After drilling pilot holes, drive 1⅝-inch screws through the slats into the frames. Use two screws in each end of every slat. (Drive screws into the center support, too.)

6. Join the side frames to the seat assembly.

The seat is joined to the side frames by 1⅝-inch screws driven through the rails and posts into the legs. The construction of the chair allows you to fine-tune the seat's height and rake before you drive any screws, however. The *Side View* provides some positioning measurements to use as a starting point.

Set the seat assembly on its side on a couple of sawhorses. Set a side frame on it, aligning it as indicated in the *Side View*. Clamp the two assemblies together with C-clamps, speed clamps, or the like. Turn the unit over and position and clamp the second side frame.

Set the clamped-together chair on its feet and try it out. Make adjustments. Raise or lower the seat. Tilt it back a bit more. Make it more erect. When you are happy with the way the chair "sits," drill the pilot holes and drive the screws. Drive two screws each through the front of the rail into the front leg, through the rail's tail into the back leg, and through the posts into the arm-leg lap joint.

Setting the height and rake of the seat in the chair is a seat-of-the-pants process. After the seat assembly and the leg assemblies are glued and set, you can clamp these parts together. Use a clamp at each of four attachment points. Then sit in the chair and see if it is comfortable. Raise or lower the seat; rake the seat forward and back. With each adjustment, sit in the chair and see how it feels.

7. Apply a finish.

Do any touch-up sanding necessary, and wipe the resulting dust from the wood with a tack cloth. Be sure all exposed edges are radiused.

Apply at least three coats of the spar varnish with a high-quality, fine-bristle varnish brush. Coat all the surfaces, including the underside of the chair or settee. Take particular care to coat any exposed end grain. Remember that with spar varnish, many thin coats add up to a better, more enduring finish than a couple of thick coats.

8. Make the cushions.

Cut a 38-inch piece of 45-inch-wide fabric for the chair cushion cover. The pattern, if any, should parallel the larger dimension. Fold the piece once across the long dimension, with the back of the fabric exposed. Stitch a seam along the 38-inch dimension, ½ inch from the edge. Turn the resulting tube right-side out, so the fabric's face is now on the outside, and center the seam on the bottom.

Flatten the tube and sew two seams across it, as shown, 19 inches and 20½ inches from one end. These seams create two separate seat-cushion compartments.

Turn under the fabric edges at both ends of the cover and hem them.

Cut the cushions from 1-inch-thick foam rubber. The seat is 21 inches by 16 inches; the back is 21 inches by 18 inches.

Stuff the foam cushions into the covers. Pin the ends of the covers shut with a row of straight pins about 1 inch from the hemmed edge of the covers—you may have to temporarily bunch up the foam to get the pins in. This allows enough room to guide the layers of fabric under the foot of the sewing machine. Fold in the corners

SEWING CHAIR CUSHION

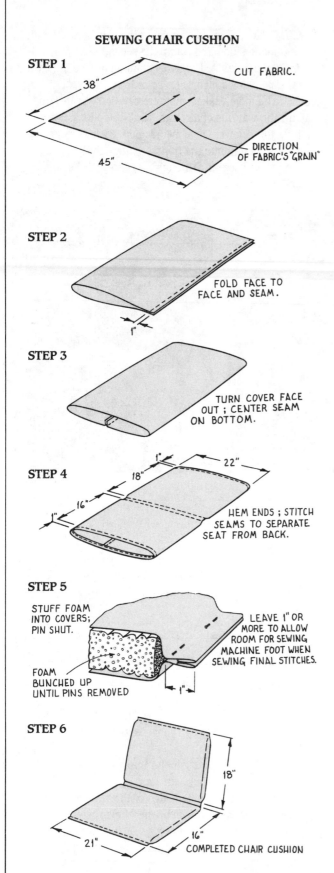

STEP 1
38"
45"
CUT FABRIC.
DIRECTION OF FABRIC'S "GRAIN"

STEP 2
FOLD FACE TO FACE AND SEAM.
1"

STEP 3
TURN COVER FACE OUT; CENTER SEAM ON BOTTOM.

STEP 4
1"
22"
18"
16"
1"
HEM ENDS; STITCH SEAMS TO SEPARATE SEAT FROM BACK.

STEP 5
STUFF FOAM INTO COVERS; PIN SHUT.
FOAM BUNCHED UP UNTIL PINS REMOVED
LEAVE 1" OR MORE TO ALLOW ROOM FOR SEWING MACHINE FOOT WHEN SEWING FINAL STITCHES.
1"

STEP 6
18"
21"
16"
COMPLETED CHAIR CUSHION

of the top and bottom layers of fabric about 1¼ inches. Sew a line of stitches through the hemmed edges of both layers of fabric, closing the ends of the covers. Remove the pins, allowing the foam to unbunch. Place the cushion on the chair.

The sequence is much the same in making the settee cushion, except that you must begin with two pieces of fabric 43 inches by 38 inches. Lay one on top of the other, face to face, and sew seams along both 38-inch dimensions, ½ inch in from the edges. This will form a 42-inch-wide by 38-inch-long tube. Turn the tube right-side out, with the seams on either side, and continue as in making the chair cushion. Stitch the two seams that form the cushion compartments, cut and insert the cushions, and sew the cover closed.

SEWING SETTEE CUSHION

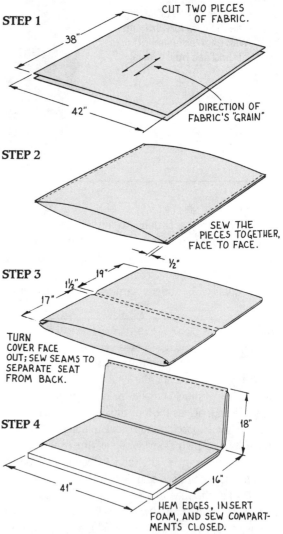

STEP 1
38"
42"
CUT TWO PIECES OF FABRIC.
DIRECTION OF FABRIC'S "GRAIN"

STEP 2
SEW THE PIECES TOGETHER, FACE TO FACE.
½"

STEP 3
19"
1½"
17"
TURN COVER FACE OUT; SEW SEAMS TO SEPARATE SEAT FROM BACK.

STEP 4
18"
16"
41"
HEM EDGES, INSERT FOAM, AND SEW COMPARTMENTS CLOSED.

VINEYARD ENSEMBLE

Classy, Comfortable, Cushioned Cedar Seating

After toiling in the vineyards all day, this is the sort of cushy seating you deserve. Deep, soft cushions and a footrest. You may never move again.

VINEYARD ENSEMBLE SETTEE AND CHAIR WITH OTTOMAN

After working hard in the yard and garden, or playing hard on the court, you deserve a break—and a comfortable place to sit while enjoying the fresh air. This smart ensemble fills the bill perfectly. The chair and matching ottoman offer the cushiness of a living-room–bound Barcalounger. The whole set reflects the refinement of indoor furniture, while retaining the clean lines and distinctive design of a custom-made patio ensemble. Imagine yourself . . . nested in the chair or settee . . . feet up . . . the Sunday paper and a tumbler of chilled orange juice on the table at your side. . . .

Get the picture? Build the set!

SHOPPING LIST—CHAIR AND OTTOMAN

LUMBER

2 pcs. 4 × 4 × 8' clear western red cedar
2 pcs. 4 × 4 × 10' clear western red cedar
1 pc. 1" dia. × 48" birch dowel

HARDWARE AND SUPPLIES

4 pcs. #6 × 3" galvanized drywall-type screws
Resorcinol glue

FABRIC AND NOTIONS

3⅓ yd. muslin, min. 31" wide (chair cushions)
1½ yd. muslin, min. 31" wide (ottoman cushion)
1 spool matching thread

FABRIC AND NOTIONS—CONTINUED

3⅓ yd. upholstery fabric, min. 31" wide (chair slipcovers)
1½ yd. upholstery fabric, min. 31" wide (ottoman slipcover)
1 spool matching upholstery thread
3 pcs. ¾" × 23" hook-and-loop tape
8 lb. shredded foam

FINISH

Leave natural, or apply clear exterior finish

SHOPPING LIST—SETTEE

LUMBER

2 pcs. 4 × 4 × 12' clear western red cedar
1 pc. 4 × 4 × 10' clear western red cedar

HARDWARE AND SUPPLIES

4 pcs. #6 × 3" galvanized drywall-type screws
Resorcinol glue

FABRIC AND NOTIONS

6⅔ yd. muslin, min. 31" wide (cushions)
1 spool matching thread

FABRIC AND NOTIONS—CONTINUED

6⅔ yd. upholstery fabric, min. 31" wide (slipcovers)
1 spool matching upholstery thread
2 pcs. ¾" × 23" hook-and-loop tape
5 lb. shredded foam

FINISH

Leave natural, or apply clear exterior finish

CUTTING LIST—CHAIR AND OTTOMAN

PIECE	NUMBER	THICKNESS	WIDTH	LENGTH	MATERIAL
Back legs	2	2½"	3"	36"	Cedar
Arms	2	1"	3½"	31"*	Cedar
Hand grips	2	¾"	1"	3½"	Cedar scraps
Front legs	2	3½"	3½"	18"*	Cedar
Side rails	2	1½"	3½"	24"	Cedar
Front rail	1	1½"	3½"	26½"	Cedar
Back slats	6	1"	3¼"	26½"	Cedar
Seat slats	4	1"	3¼"	28"	Cedar
Ottoman legs	4	3½"	3½"	12"*	Cedar
Ottoman front rails	2	1½"	3½"	26"	Cedar
Ottoman side rails	2	1½"	3½"	21½"	Cedar
Ottoman slats	4	1"	3¼"	27½"	Cedar
Ottoman handles	2	1" dia.	22"		Birch dowel

*Dimensions of piece before tapers or shapes are cut

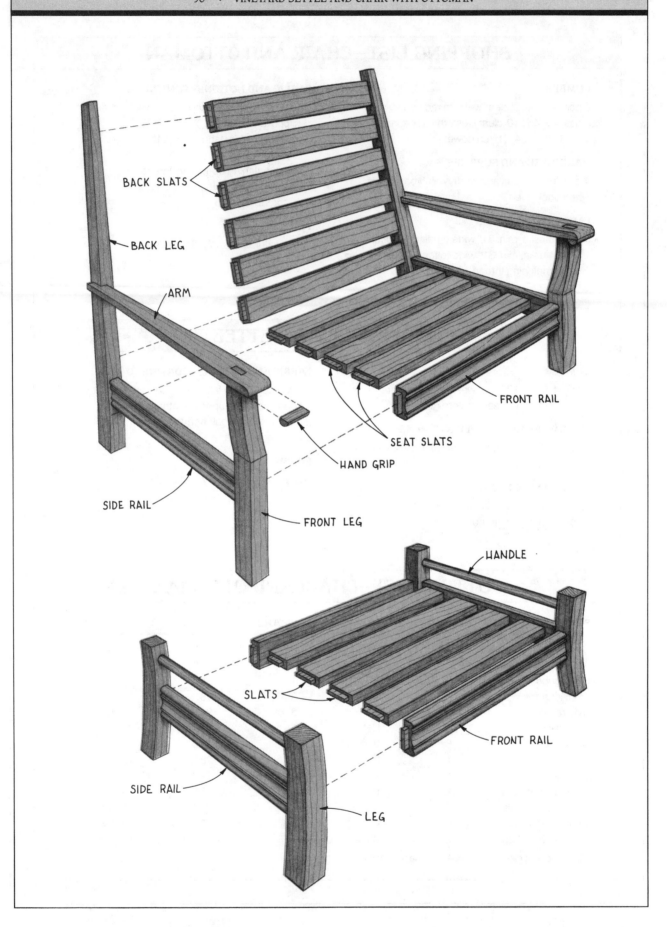

BACK SLATS

BACK LEG

ARM

SIDE RAIL

FRONT LEG

HAND GRIP

SEAT SLATS

FRONT RAIL

HANDLE

SLATS

FRONT RAIL

SIDE RAIL

LEG

CUTTING LIST—SETTEE

PIECE	NUMBER	THICKNESS	WIDTH	LENGTH	MATERIAL
Back legs	2	2½"	3"	36"	Cedar
Arms	2	1"	3½"	31"*	Cedar
Hand grips	2	¾"	1"	3½"	Cedar
Front legs	2	3½"	3½"	18"*	Cedar
Side rails	2	1½"	3½"	24"	Cedar
Front rail	1	1½"	3½"	51½"	Cedar
Back slats	6	1"	3¼"	51½"	Cedar
Seat slats	4	1"	3¼"	53"	Cedar

*Dimensions of piece before tapers or shapes are cut

CUTTING DIAGRAM—CHAIR AND OTTOMAN

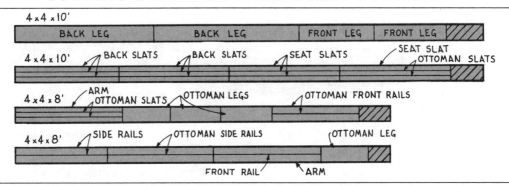

CUTTING DIAGRAM—SETTEE

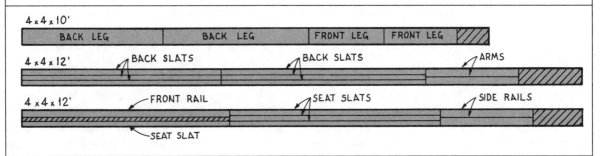

Builder's Notes

The Vineyard Ensemble is one of the more challenging projects in this book. If you tackle it, you must deal with several different band saw operations, an unusual table saw setup, and the cutting of more than three dozen mortise-and-tenon joints. And if you make your own cushions, there's *sewing* involved, too.

Your reward is a set of outdoor furniture that, if you *could* buy it, would cost a couple of thousand dollars.

As with the Mahogany Ensemble on page 51, which includes a chair *and* a settee, the settee is just a wider version of the chair. The side frame assemblies are identical; for the settee, you simply cut the slats and front rail longer (compare the cutting lists). Although the photos on the following pages show building procedures for the settee, the construction sequence and techniques are the same for both pieces.

Materials. We chose to make the project of western red cedar for its natural beauty and resistance to decay. We made the ensemble from 4 × 4s. From this we resawed the boards needed for the slats, rails, and arms.

PATTERNS

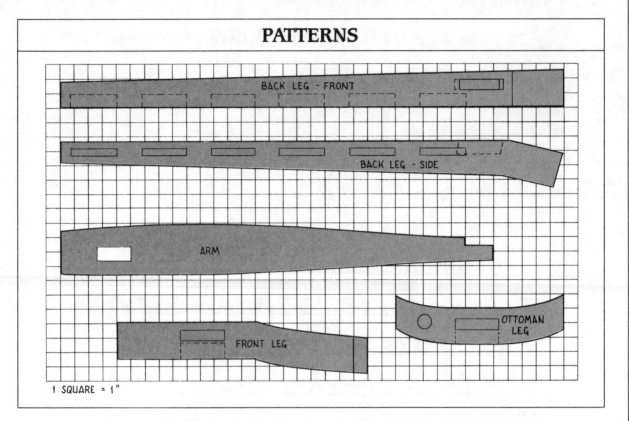

1 SQUARE = 1"

If you want to avoid the resawing, you can buy 2-by stock for the rails, 5/4 (five-quarter) stock (usually stocked as decking) for the slats and arms.

Though the cedar *is* naturally decay resistant, this is not really the sort of furniture you'd thoughtlessly leave out in the rain. A protected patio or porch is a more appropriate setting. A finish of some sort is appropriate. You can use a clear penetrating oil finish. If more outdoor protection is desired, apply either a clear water repellent or an exterior preservative stain.

An upholsterer can make the cushions for you, but they're easy enough to make yourself if you have basic sewing skills.

All the materials you need are to be had at a fabric or upholstery shop. You need fabric to make a cover for the cushions (muslin is durable, relatively inexpensive, and widely available), as well as a fabric (probably colored or patterned) for slipcovers. And you need material to fill the cushions. Ultimately, we used shredded foam. Slabs of foam rubber by themselves—we tried them—give the cushions an unappealingly angular look and an uninvitingly firm feel. We tried cutting the foam slabs slightly undersized, then wrapping them with polyester batting to soften the sharp edges. But eventually, we settled on the shredded stuffing because it produced cushions that were a balm for sore bodies.

Tools and techniques. This is a project for the well-equipped shop. It is very much a band saw project, though the table saw and the drill press are also key tools.

The band saw is used for the obvious operations, such as cutting the arms and legs. But it is also used to resaw the 4 × 4 stock into 1-inch-thick arms and slats and 1½-inch-thick rails. No other tool will perform these tasks as well.

You use the table saw to cut the wide coves in the rails of each piece. Setting up for the cove cuts on the table saw is a trial-and-error process; it may take as much time to set up the saw and fence to get the cove cut just right as it will to make the actual cuts.

Finally, you have to master the mortise-and-tenon joint. There are 28 mortise-and-tenon joints in the chair, another 16 in the ottoman. We cut the tenons on the table saw, the mortises using a mortising attachment on the drill press. The tenons can also be cut on the band saw or using a router. The mortise can be roughed out with a drill and finished with a mallet and chisel. But if you have a drill press, this ensemble might be just the excuse you need to justify the purchase of a mortising attachment.

A note on overall planning is in order. Because some of the setups are so difficult to duplicate, it's wise to make all possible use of them before breaking them down.

Take the cove-cutting setup, for example. The rails on all the furniture pieces have identical face profiles. Once you've set up the table saw to make cove cuts for one piece of furniture, it makes sense to cut coves for any of the other pieces you intend to make. But to do that, you have to have all the rails rough-cut on the table saw. So to avoid using the same machine to do two things at once, apply a production-line method. Decide ahead of time all the pieces you are going to make. Organize the parts and the routines, so you can perform all like operations at one time. Rough-cut the parts for all the furniture pieces at one time, cut all the mortises, cut all the coves, and so forth.

It will save you time in the long run.

1. Rough the parts from the 4 × 4 stock. Crosscut the parts following the *Cutting Diagram* and the "Cutting List," then resaw the appropriate blanks to produce the thinner pieces, such as the arms, rails, and slats. *Don't taper or shape any pieces yet.*

Few saws for crosscutting have the capacity to cut a 4 × 4 in a single pass. You'll probably have to mark each cut on opposing faces and make two passes to complete the cuts. A circular saw or radial arm saw is good for the job.

With the stock reduced to manageable lengths, resawing the stock for arms, slats, and rails is a band saw operation. After the parts are resawed, use a hand plane, a light cut on a jointer, or a sander to smooth the surfaces. The soft cedar will cut fast, so be especially careful if you are using a belt sander.

2. Shape the face profile on the rails. Make the first cuts with a router equipped with a ½-inch beading bit. See the *Rail Cross Section Detail* for the location of the bead cuts. Make trial cuts on scrap to perfect the setup, then cut beads on all the rails. (Save your "best" scrap piece for testing the cove setup.) Then rout a ¼-inch-radius roundover on the inner edges of the rail, as shown.

To complete the face profile, machine a cove on the rails using the table saw. To do this, you must feed the workpiece over the saw blade at an angle. Only a tiny amount of material can be removed at one time, so cut the cove in a series of passes.

The trickiest part is the setup.

Draw the desired cove profile on the butt end of a scrap. (Size the cove so that there is a ⅛-inch flat between the bead and the cove; the depth of the cove is not critical.) Move the saw's rip fence out of the way (or remove it completely). Set the depth of cut to equal the maximum depth of the cove. Align a straight board—to serve as an auxiliary fence—more or less diagonally across the saw table, just in front of the blade.

Adjust the shape of the cove by changing the angle of the auxiliary fence: Moving the fence more parallel to the blade will give a narrower cove at a given blade height, while moving the fence more perpendicular to the blade will give a wider cove at the same blade height.

With this in mind, set the scrap behind the blade and against the fence. Sight along the auxiliary fence at table height, adjusting the angle until the blade just obscures

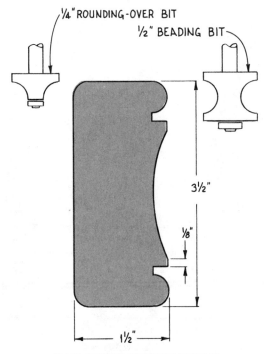

RAIL CROSS SECTION DETAIL

CHAIR PLAN VIEWS

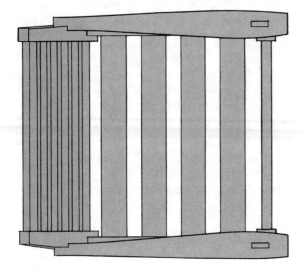

TOP VIEW

TOOL LIST

Band saw	Router
Block plane	¼ " rounding-over bit
Circular saw	½ " beading bit
Clamps	Sander(s)
Drill	Sandpaper
Pilot hole bit	Sawhorses
Drill press	Screwdriver
Hollow-chisel mortising	Sewing machine
attachment	Table saw
Hand plane	Dado cutter
Mallet	Miter gauge
Marking gauge	Tack cloth
Paintbrush	Tape measure
Pipe clamps	Try square

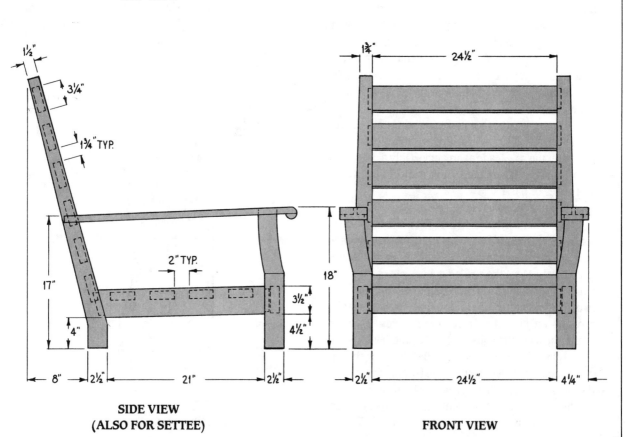

SIDE VIEW
(ALSO FOR SETTEE)

FRONT VIEW

the marks on the end of the scrap. Clamp the fence in position.

Now test your setup. Crank down the blade so that it cuts only about 1/16 inch deep and start cutting. After each pass, raise the blade about 1/16 inch. Your test isn't done until you achieve the maximum depth desired. This is because raising the blade on most table saws moves it backward or forward at the same time. There's no guarantee the center of thc cut will remain in the same place, so you can't be sure whether the cove you want is the cove you'll get until you've carried the process through to completion.

If your test proves the setup to be right on, then start cutting coves in the rails. If not, then unclamp the auxiliary fence and make adjustments to the angle, based on whether the cove needs to be wider or narrower.

After drawing the cove profile on the end of the rail, position the rail and auxiliary fence as shown. "Eyeball" the blade's profile against the marked cove profile, adjusting the fence angle to make the cut wider or narrower. The space between the auxiliary fence and the blade dictates, of course, where the cove will be in relation to the edge of the workpiece.

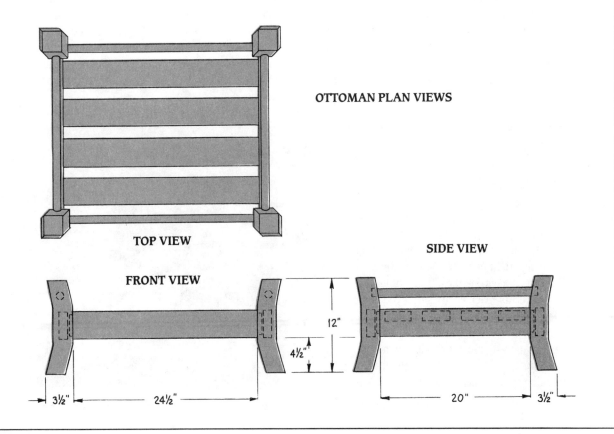

OTTOMAN PLAN VIEWS

TOP VIEW

FRONT VIEW

SIDE VIEW

12"

4½"

3½"

24½"

20"

3½"

Feed the rail across the blade, beaded side down. It's best to make several light passes, raising the blade a bit each time, until full depth is reached, rather than trying to remove all the stock in a single pass. Attempting to cut the cove in one pass will probably stall the machine and could damage your saw motor.

3. **Lay out the legs.** The front, back, and ottoman legs have mortises that must be laid out and cut before you completely shape the legs. Especially if you are using a mortising attachment on a drill press to make the mortises, the stock must be square to properly perform the operation. Note that the chair legs are *mirror images,* not duplicates. As you lay out these legs on the 4 × 4 stock, be sure you lay out a right leg and a left leg. Note that while the chair legs are mirror images, all four ottoman legs are identical.

Lay out the mortises and curves at the same time. For the front legs, enlarge the pattern and make a template (including a hole for the mortise) of cardboard or thin plywood. Set the two leg blanks side by side in front of you. Trace the template on one blank. Flip the template over, and trace it on an adjoining face of the same blank. Repeat the process on the second blank, but be sure you lay out a *mirror image* of the first blank. Finally, lay out the tenon for the arm on each leg. As shown in the *Front Leg Detail,* the tenon is located ½ inch from the outside face of the legs.

The ottoman legs should be laid out from the pattern. Enlarge it and make a template, from which you can lay out the legs.

TIP

To help establish and maintain the proper left-leg/right-leg orientation when laying out the back legs, cut just their front profiles. Then position them as shown to lay out the slat mortises. At this point, either leg could be a right or a left. Marking the mortise locations makes one the left, the other the right; this approach ensures that you end up with a left leg and a right leg. It also helps you expedite uniform mortise layouts. Use a combination square to transfer the mortise locations from one leg to the other, and a marking gauge to scribe the mortise sides.

4. **Lay out the mortises in the rails.** Lay out the locations for the mortises on the (chair and ottoman) side rails, as shown in the *Rail Layouts* drawing. To ensure that the slats fit squarely between the rails and at a uniform setback from the edge, lay out each pair of rails at the same time. Use a square to mark mortise locations across both rails at the same time, then scribe the sides of the mortises with a marking gauge.

RAIL LAYOUTS

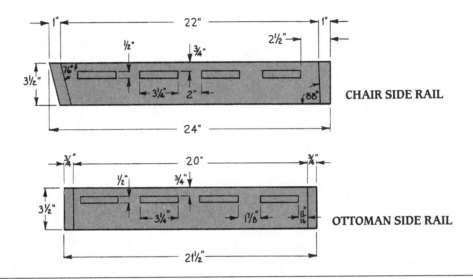

CHAIR SIDE RAIL

OTTOMAN SIDE RAIL

5. **Cut the tenons on the slats and rails.** On both ends of each slat, lay out and cut a tenon ½ inch thick by 3¼ inches wide by 1 inch long (the same width as the slat itself—there are no shoulders on the narrow ends of the tenons).

Lay out and cut the tenons on the ends of each rail to the dimensions shown in the *Rail Tenon Detail*. The shoulders of the chair side rail tenons are NOT square (see the *Rail Layouts*). The shoulders of the front tenons are cut at an 88 degree angle, the shoulders of the rear tenons at a 76 degree angle. The end of the rear tenon should be cut parallel to the shoulders, but the end of the front tenon can be left square.

We cut all the tenons using a dado cutter in a table saw. Set the depth of cut to match the width of the shoulder. Position the rip fence so the distance from the *outside* of the cutter to the fence face equals the length of the tenon. Butt the end of the workpiece against the fence

RAIL TENON DETAIL

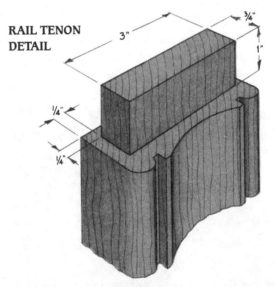

and guide it over the cutter with the miter gauge. Make as many passes as necessary to form the tenon.

6. **Cut all the mortises.** By waiting until now to cut the mortises, you can set up a more efficient production line to finish them all at once. Also, since the tenons have been cut, you can test fit them in their mortises.

The standard mortise-cutting technique is to rough out the mortises with a drill bit slightly smaller in diameter than the finished width of the mortise. Then you cut to the layout lines with a chisel. When working with a drill press, clamp a makeshift fence to the table, so you can position the mortises uniformly and accurately. And set the depth stop, so that all the mortises are roughed to a uniform depth—usually about 1/16 inch deeper than the tenons are long.

We chose another approach. We cut all the mortises using a mortising attachment on a drill press. This device, which combines a chisel with a drill bit, "bores" a square hole. This eliminates the handwork of squaring each mortise with a chisel.

Note: The mortises (in the legs) for the chair side

rails are somewhat out-of-the-ordinary. See the *Side View* and the patterns. In the front leg blanks, these mortises must be cut deeper than the others, since the true depth must be measured not from the surface you are working with at this point, but from the final profile. In the back legs, the mortises must be cut at an angle. Tilt the drill press table to the correct degree (or cut a wedge to fit underneath the leg to achieve the same effect). Stand a try square on the lower section of the leg. When the blade is parallel to the bit, the angle is correct.

7. Cut out the legs. Use the band saw. Cutting the back legs is pretty straightforward. Rest the leg on its back and saw the side taper. Then turn the leg onto the inner face and cut the back profile.

The front legs are less straightforward. First, you must cut the tenon for the arm, then you must shape the leg with compound cuts. Cut two opposing sides first—sides 1 and 2 in the *Front Leg Detail*. Then, tape the waste pieces back to the blank—use masking tape. Cut the other sides—sides 3 and 4 in the illustration. Remove the waste and any remaining tape.

The ottoman legs also require compound cuts, and they should be cut in the same manner as the front legs.

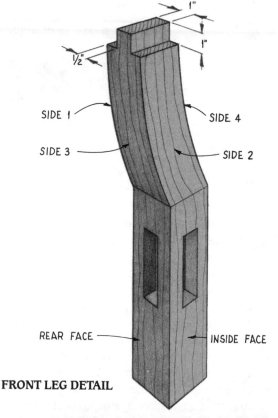

FRONT LEG DETAIL

Cutting the "double profile" front legs requires cutting along the layout lines on one face, then rolling the workpiece 90 degrees and cutting along the lines on the second face. *Above:* To provide a square, steady, and safe bearing surface for making the second series of cuts, you must tape the waste from the first series of cuts back in place, then cut. *Right:* When all the cuts are done, remove all the waste and peel away tape scraps.

SETTEE PLAN VIEWS

TOP VIEW

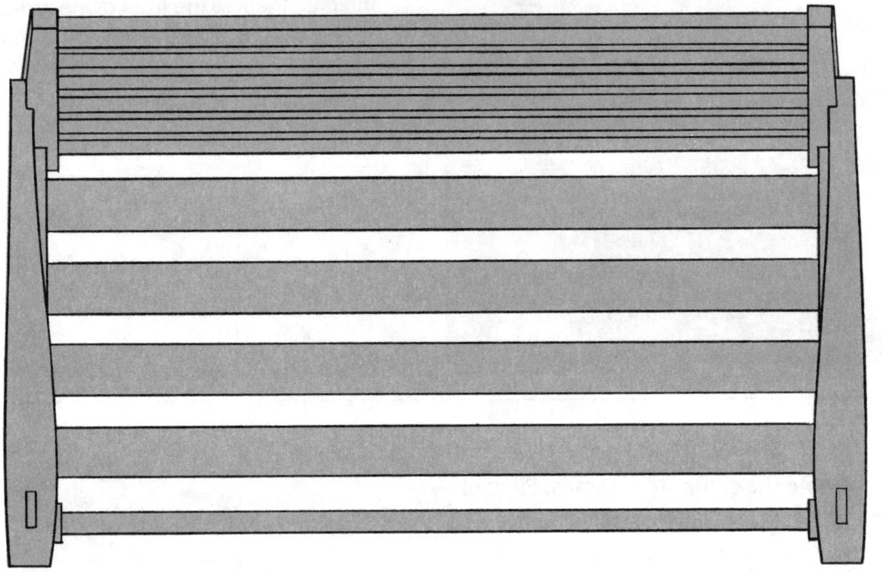

FRONT VIEW

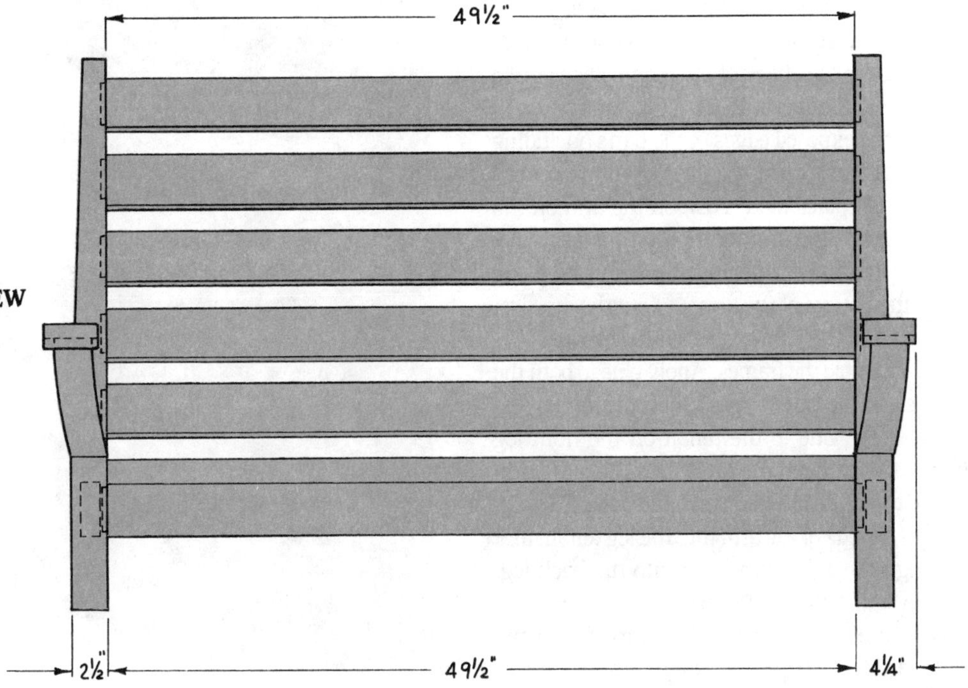

49½"

2½"   49½"   4¼"

8. **Cut out the arms.** Enlarge the pattern for the arms and transfer it to the roughly sized board set aside for the arms. Cut out two ¾ inch by 1 inch by 3½ inch hand grips from scrap, and round the shapes on the band saw. Glue the grips to the underside of the front edge of the arms. After the glue sets, cut the arms on the band saw. Make the cuts with the grip facing up, and cut slightly outside the marked layout lines. Round-over the front edge of the arms and grips on the band saw or with a rasp. Sand the completed arms.

Cut out the shape of the hand grips on the band saw and glue them to the front of the arm piece, as shown. Spring clamps hold the grips in place while the glue dries.

9. **Assemble the chair side frames.** First, dry assemble the legs and rails to make two side frames. The joint between the side rail and the front leg has a slight misfit built into it—the top and bottom of the tenon slope up into a mortise that has no slope. The cedar is soft enough to make a force-fit possible. If you don't want to force the fit, give the top cheek of the tenon a lick or two with a block plane to taper it to fit.

Radius all the exposed edges of the parts (including the arms) with a router and a ¼-inch rounding-over bit.

Fit the arm in place next. Position the arm on the side frame and mark the arm location on the back leg. Then mark the mortise by tracing the tenon atop the front leg onto the bottom of the arm. Cut out the mortise, and check the fit of the joint. Adjust if necessary.

Now, disassemble the frames. Apply glue to both the frame mortises and the tenons, reassemble the frames and clamp them. Apply glue to the tenon on the front leg and to the mortise through the arm, then drive the arm down over the tenon. Drill a pilot hole and drive a 3-inch screw through the side of the arm into the leg tenon, and another through the side of the arm into the back leg. Leave the side frame clamped overnight.

If you don't have a large supply of clamps, glue one side frame at a time.

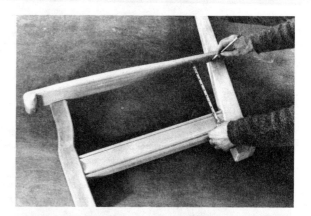

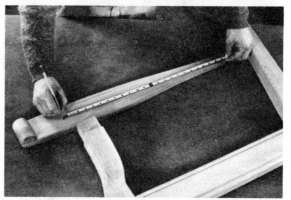

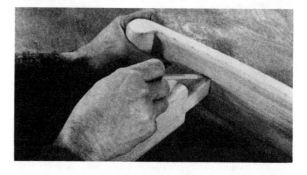

Fitting the arm to its side frame is a key part of the assembly process. *Top:* Position the arm parallel to the rail by measuring between the parts with a tape at front to back. Mark the arm position on the back leg. *Center:* Next, measure from the mark on the leg to the front-leg tenon, and transfer the measurement to the arm. *Bottom:* Finally, center the arm over the front leg, aligning the tenon to the mark on the arm. Trace the tenon onto the arm.

When gluing up the side assembly, a little masking tape can serve as extra hands, holding the cauls—scrap blocks that prevent the clamp jaws from marring the good wood—against the legs, making it easier to apply the clamp. Cut a wedge-shaped caul to fit behind the back leg and provide a square clamping surface.

10. Complete the chair assembly. It is usually a good idea, in an assembly process like this one, to conduct a dry run. You have the opportunity to check how all the joints fit and make any necessary adjustments. You also have the chance to coordinate your movements with your helper. Yes, you probably need one for this process.

For final assembly, start with a side assembly on your bench, with the mortises up. Apply glue to the mortises of one side frame first, then to the tenons. Insert the slats into the side frame. Apply glue to the mortises in the second side assembly. Upend the first assembly to insert the slat tenons into the mortises in the second side assembly.

(The reason you do it this way is to keep the glue from running out of the mortises and all over your project. Resorcinol glue, as you probably know, is runny and stains whatever it touches a dark maroon. You don't want to apply too much to the tenons, for if they are properly snug, assembly will "squeegee" the glue off the tenons' cheeks and onto their shoulders. Once there, it will squeeze out and make a mess. So you want to apply the glue in the mortise, but you don't want it to drip out on the project or on you during assembly. Keep the mortises oriented so the glue can't drip out.)

Once the project is assembled and all the tenons are set firmly into their mortises, use one pipe clamp or bar clamp to clamp the back. Carefully set the project on its feet and apply additional clamps to pull all the joints tight. Keep the clamps on overnight.

After the glue has set, trim the front-leg tenons flush with the top of the arms.

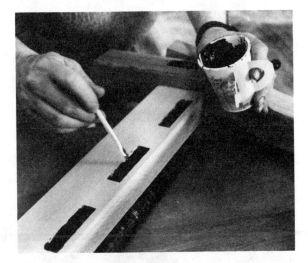

Assembly begins with the application of an even coat of glue on the sides of the mortises. A paper cup is a good mixing pot for the two-part resorcinol glue, and an inexpensive acid brush is a good reusable applicator.

TIP

During the dry run, as you fit each tenon to a particular mortise, lightly mark a number on both parts at the joint, so you won't accidentally mix up their locations when you disassemble the pieces for gluing. Cedar is very soft, so don't pencil too heavily.

How do you get all those slats fitted into all those mortises? It isn't as hard as you might think. *Top:* One by one, coat the tenons on the front rail and the slats with glue, then push them into the mortises in one side assembly. *Center left:* When that's done, steady the second side with scraps under the legs, and upend the assembly with the slats and rail. This will teach you the value of snug joints; it they aren't snug, the slats will drop out. *Center right:* Try to align as many of the tenons as you can over their mortises as you lower the project onto the second side assembly. *Bottom left:* A good approach is to cock the assembly slightly, working the front rail into position first, then the slat closest to it, then the next slat, and the next. Try not to smear glue on the legs and side rail as you line up the joints. Resorcinol has a long open time, so you needn't rush. *Bottom right:* After all the tenons have dropped into place, apply a single clamp to the back, primarily to hold the slats between the back legs while you lift the project and set it on its feet. Then apply more clamps and tighten them to close the joints.

TIP

If you don't have enough long clamps to clamp the side assemblies together (a likely possibility if you're making the settee), you can make one long clamp by joining two shorter ones, as shown here.

11. Assemble the ottoman. If you choose to buy standard 1-inch birch dowel for the handles, it can be cut to length and stained to match the color of the red cedar. If you have a lathe, you can turn the handles from cedar scrap left over from cutting the slats.

Dry assemble the parts to check the fit of the joints, and make any adjustments before proceeding. When you're sure everything fits well, assemble the ottoman with resorcinol glue and clamp overnight to dry.

12. Apply a finish. Sand all surfaces smooth and apply the finish of your choice. We recommend a water repellent or a clear penetrating exterior finish.

Cushions

If you're handy with a sewing machine, making these cushions for the chair, matching ottoman, and settee will be a snap. If sewing is new to you, this is a good project to get you started. All the seams are straight and simple. Get a friend to show you how to thread the sewing machine's bobbin and needle, and how to stitch a straight line—that's all there is to it.

The cushions are designed to be protected with slipcovers. For the cushions themselves, use muslin, as we did. For the slipcovers, buy upholstery fabric that will be heavy enough to wear well and that is pleasing to your eye. Depending upon the weight of the slipcover fabric, you may need to buy a heavy gauge needle for the sewing machine, and heavy upholstery thread, too—check with the clerk at the fabric store for guidance.

The seat and back cushions for the settee are the same size as those for the chair—just make two of each.

1. Stitch the cushions. For each chair/settee cushion, cut two pieces of muslin that are 31 inches by 58¾ inches. For the ottoman cushion, cut the muslin to 31 inches by 52¾ inches.

Do one cushion at a time. Hem the ends of the muslin. To do this, fold over about ½ inch of cloth, bringing the good, outside surface of the fabric—known as the "right" side in sewing parlance—over the less attractive, less colorful side that will end up inside the finished cushion—known as the "wrong" side. Make another ½-inch fold over the first fold. Sew along the center of the fold.

After hemming both ends, fold the cloth in half, wrong sides together, bringing the hemmed edges together.

CUSHION SEWING SEQUENCE

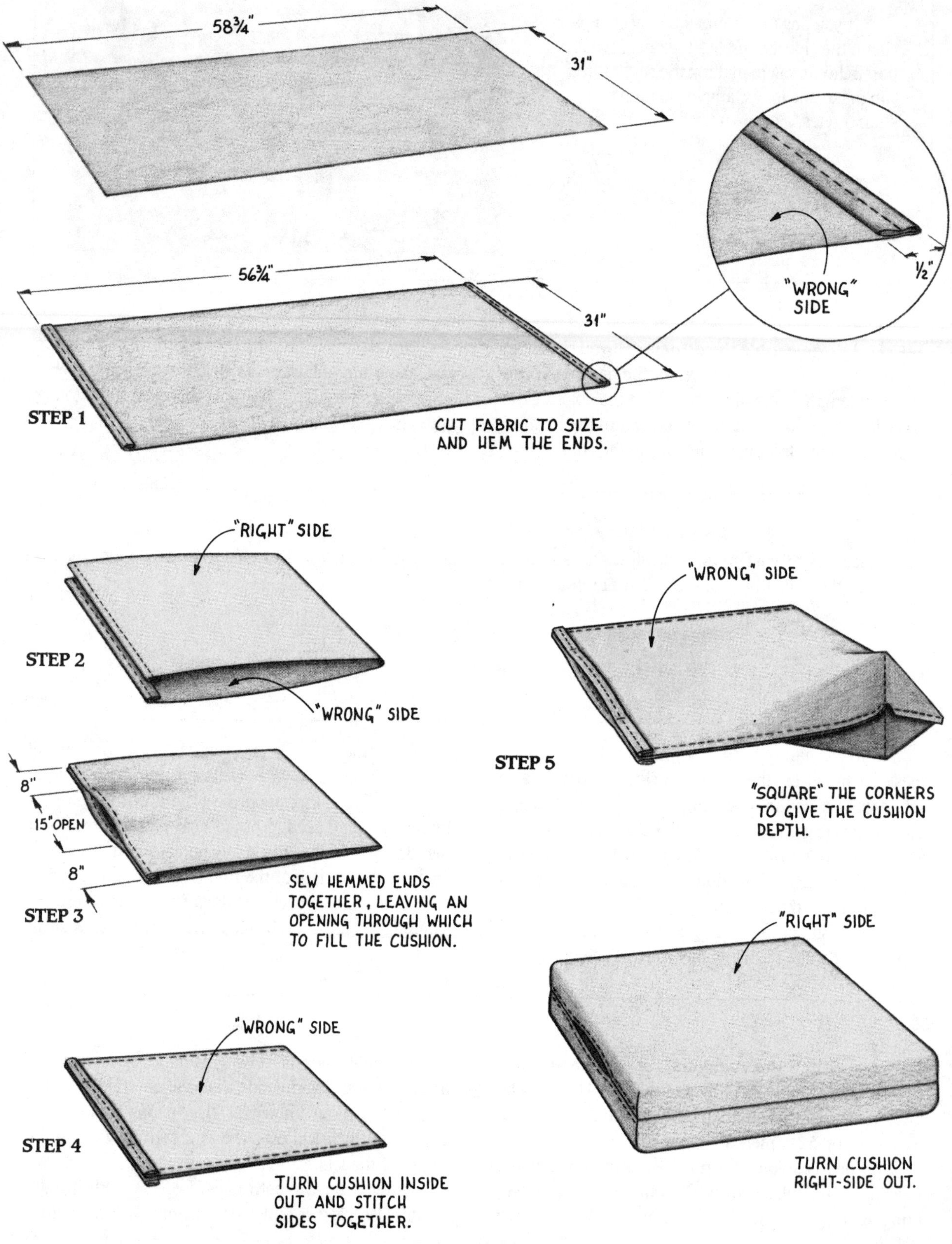

58¾"

31"

½"

"WRONG" SIDE

56¾"

31"

STEP 1

CUT FABRIC TO SIZE
AND HEM THE ENDS.

"RIGHT" SIDE

STEP 2

"WRONG" SIDE

8"

15" OPEN

8"

STEP 3

SEW HEMMED ENDS
TOGETHER, LEAVING AN
OPENING THROUGH WHICH
TO FILL THE CUSHION.

"WRONG" SIDE

STEP 5

"SQUARE" THE CORNERS
TO GIVE THE CUSHION
DEPTH.

"WRONG" SIDE

STEP 4

TURN CUSHION INSIDE
OUT AND STITCH
SIDES TOGETHER.

"RIGHT" SIDE

TURN CUSHION
RIGHT-SIDE OUT.

Stitch the hemmed edges together at the ends, leaving the center open; this is the opening through which you will stuff the cushion.

Now turn the cover inside out, so the right sides are together. Using a ½-inch seam allowance (which means aligning the seam ½ inch from the edge of the cloth), sew the unhemmed edges together to close the open side. The result is a flat pouch.

To give the cushion depth, sew a short seam at each corner, perpendicular to those already sewn. To do this,

pick up the "pouch" and separate the two layers of fabric near a corner, pulling them away from one another. Fold the fabric flat and neat in a new plane; the previously sewn seam should bisect the corner, as shown. Stitch a seam across the corner, forming a triangle; the length of this seam will determine the thickness of the cushion. It should be about 5 inches long. Repeat for each corner of each cushion.

Turn the cover right-side out, and it is ready to be stuffed.

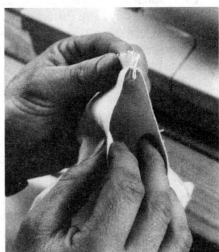

Left: The sewing required to make the cushions is as simple as stitching a straight seam on the sewing machine. *Right:* After hemming the ends of the fabric, fold the cloth so the hems overlap. Sew through both hems, along the hem stitches, forming a seam that turns the strip of cloth into a loop. This seam is on the surface, and you'll want this to be on the back of the cushion.

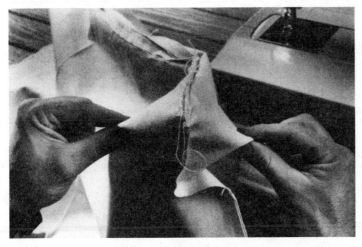

Squaring the corners of the cushions is easier to do than to describe. *Left:* As shown, you pull the layers of the cushion apart to create a plane perpendicular to the seams sewn so far. *Right:* After smoothing out the wrinkles, you stitch diagonally across the corner, thereby establishing cushion depth. The farther from the corner you position the seam, the longer it will be, and the fatter the cushion will be.

2. Stuff the cushions. The shredded foam we used was packaged in 1-pound bags, and we used about 2½ bags per cushion.

Open the package, fit the opening inside the cushion, then shake the stuffing out of the package and into the cushion. Fill each cushion to the girth you desire, but remember that you must be able to pinch the opening closed and stitch it on the sewing machine.

When you have stuffed the cushions and sewn them closed, the basic cushion is completed. Although you can use them like this, the covers will get dirty pretty quickly, and they'll be hard to clean. Better you should make slipcovers for them.

3. Stitch the slipcovers. The slipcovers are made in the same way as the cushions, except that you use hook-and-loop strips (Velcro) to close the openings rather than sewing them closed. Moreover, you'll probably want to use colored or patterned upholstery fabric.

Cut the slipcover fabric for each cushion. The cut sizes for the slipcovers match the sizes for the muslin given in step 1. Hem the edges as you did in making the covers.

Cut a 23-inch length of hook-and-loop tape (each length has a hook strip and a loop strip) for each cushion. Separate the hook strips from the loop strips. Sew a hook strip on the wrong side of the fabric, centered along the hemmed edge. Sew a loop strip on the right side of the fabric, centered on the opposite hemmed edge, as shown.

The side seams of the cushion are sewn with the fabric inside out—that is, with the wrong side exposed. Turn the fabric right-sides-together and mate the hook-and-loop strips. Using a ½-inch hem allowance, sew along the (unhemmed) sides.

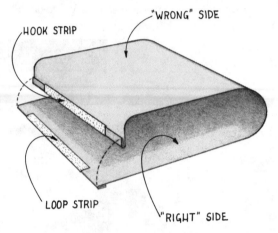

HOOK-AND-LOOP POSITION

Square the corners next. At each corner, pinch the cloth between the thumb and fingers and pull, separating the layers. Flatten the corner, align the seams atop one another, and sew the diagonal seam.

Open the hook-and-loop strip and turn the fabric right-side out.

4. Put the slipcovers on the cushions. Stuff the cushion into the slipcover, and close the hook-and-loop strips.

Now, fluff up the cushions, put them on the chair and ottoman, and try them out—aaahhhh!

VINEYARD ENSEMBLE TABLE

This small table is just the right size to keep an ice-cold drink, a plate of snacks, and a few of your favorite books or magazines within arm's reach while kicking back in the chair or settee.

Essentially a (larger) sibling to the ottoman, the table has basically the same appearance. Though more elongated, the table legs, like the ottoman legs, are made with compound cuts on the band saw. The decorative profile for the rails is identical. Again echoing the ottoman's construction, slats form a shelf beneath the top. A relatively square, fairly smooth cut flagstone (also known as a stepping or gauged stone) serves as the top.

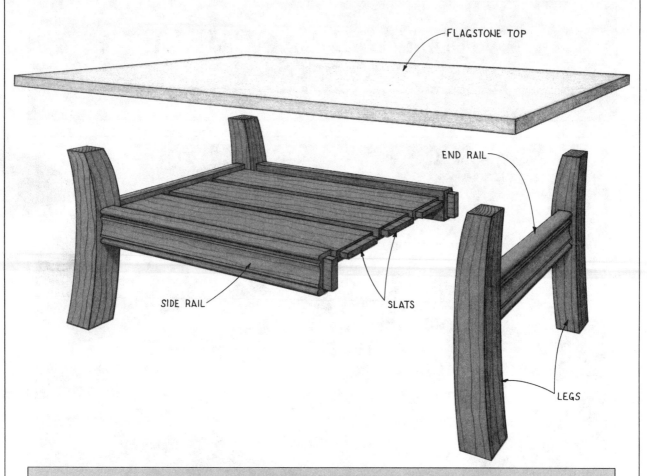

FLAGSTONE TOP

END RAIL

SIDE RAIL

SLATS

LEGS

SHOPPING LIST

LUMBER

1 pc. 4 × 4 × 12' clear western red cedar

HARDWARE AND SUPPLIES

1 flagstone, approx. 1" × 24" × 36"
Rescorcinol glue

FINISH

Leave natural, or apply clear exterior finish

CUTTING LIST

PIECE	NUMBER	THICKNESS	WIDTH	LENGTH	MATERIAL
Legs	4	3½"	3½"	17"	Cedar
Side rails	2	1½"	3½"	25½"	Cedar
End rails	2	1½"	3½"	13½"	Cedar
Slats	3	1"	3½"	26¼"	Cedar

CUTTING DIAGRAM

4 × 4 × 12'

| LEG | LEG | LEG | LEG | SIDE RAILS | END RAILS | SLATS |

PATTERN

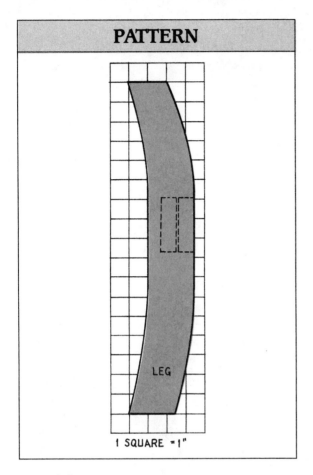

LEG

1 SQUARE = 1"

TOOL LIST

Band clamp
Band saw
Chisel
Circular saw
Drill
   Various-size wood-boring bits
Drill press
   Hollow-chisel moritising
     attachment
Hand plane
Paintbrush
Pipe clamps
Router
   ¼" rounding-over bit
   ½" beading bit
Sander(s)
Sandpaper
Sawhorses
Short bar clamps
Table saw
Tack cloth
Tape measure
Try square

Builder's Notes

A companion project to the settee and chair with ottoman that opened this chapter, the table is constructed with the same materials and uses the same tools and techniques as those earlier projects. By all means read the "Builder's Notes" accompanying the settee and chair with ottoman project on page 91.

The one item that is unique to the table is the top. Before building the table, we shopped at a landscaping center and found the flagstone you see as the tabletop. With the stone in the shop, we established the length and width of the table and went to work on the wood.

It might be most economical for you to do likewise. Buy a suitable stone for the top, and once you have it, adjust the table dimensions to suit. To alter length, simply increase or reduce the length of the side rails and slats. To change the width, you'll have to alter the width of the slats, or the space between the slats, or the number of slats, as well as the length of the end rails.

Shop for the stone at rock quarries, landscaping and gardening centers, and building supply centers.

---

1. Rough the parts from the 4 × 4 stock. Crosscut the parts following the *Cutting Diagram* and the "Cutting List," then resaw the appropriate blanks to produce the rails and slats. *Don't shape any pieces yet.*

Because few saws for crosscutting have the capacity to cut a 4 × 4 in a single pass, you'll probably have to mark opposing faces and complete each cut in two passes. Cut the stock with either a circular saw or a radial arm saw as on the chair.

With the stock reduced to manageable lengths, resawing the stock for slats and rails is a band saw operation. After the parts are resawed, use a hand plane, a light cut on a jointer, or a sander to smooth the surfaces. The soft cedar will cut fast, so be especially careful.

PLAN VIEWS

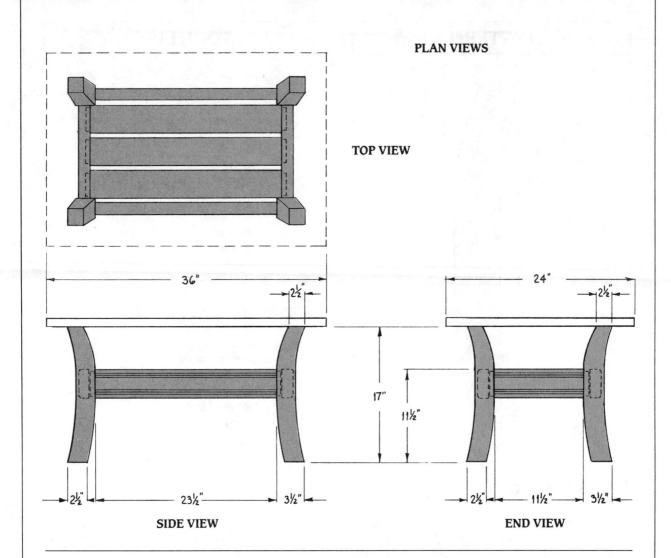

TOP VIEW

36"

2½"

24"

2½"

17"

11½"

2½" 23½" 3½"

2½" 11½" 3½"

SIDE VIEW

END VIEW

2. **Make the rails and slats.** Shape two edges of the rails with a ½-inch beading bit in a router, then machine a ¼-inch radius on the other two edges. Machine a cove on the rails with a table saw, as you did the chair and ottoman rails (see step 2 of the Vineyard Settee and Chair with Ottoman project on page 93).

Lay out and cut the tenons on both ends of each rail, as shown in the *Tenon Detail*. Then lay out the mortises in each end rail for the slats, as shown in the *End Rail Layout* drawing.

On both ends of each slat, lay out and cut a tenon ¾ inch thick by ¾ inch long by 3¼ inches wide, with a ⅛-inch shoulder on all four sides.

Cut the mortises next. We cut all the mortises using a mortising attachment on a drill press, which eliminates the handwork of squaring each mortise with a chisel. When working with a drill press, clamp a make-

TENON DETAIL

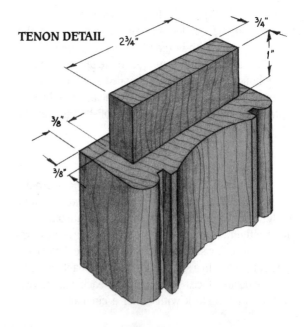

2¾" ¾" 1" ⅜" ⅜"

shift fence to the table, so you can position the mortises uniformly and accurately. And set the depth stop, so that all the mortises are roughed to a uniform depth—usually about 1/16 inch deeper than the tenons are long.

You can, of course, rough out the mortises with a drill bit slightly smaller in diameter than the mortise width. Then cut to the layout lines with a chisel.

END RAIL LAYOUT

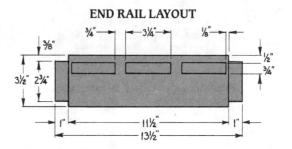

3. Make the legs. Since the legs' front and side profiles are identical, you can use the same pattern for both. Enlarge the pattern (including the size and location of the mortise), make a durable—cardboard or plywood—template, and use it to lay out the leg blanks.

Cut the mortises *before* cutting the leg profiles. Use the same techniques to mortise the legs as you did to

mortise the rails in step 2.

Next, cut the profile of each leg on the band saw. Use the same technique as for the front legs of the chair and the ottoman legs—cut two opposing sides first, reattach the waste pieces with tape, then cut the other two sides.

4. Assemble the table. Dry assemble all the parts to make sure the joints fit properly. Make any needed adjustments.

Glue the side rails between the legs to make two leg assemblies. Then, glue and clamp the three slats to the end rails. Finally, join the two leg assemblies to the end rails, and clamp the whole thing by tightening a band clamp around the four legs, even with the rails. Keep clamped overnight, or until glue has cured completely.

Lightly sand the surfaces of the table and apply the same finish used on the chair, ottoman, and/or settee.

The flagstone top doesn't need to be attached. Because of its weight, it won't blow off, and it is unlikely to be jarred off center. Simply set the stone on the tops of the legs. If necessary, trim the tops of the legs so the stone sits squarely and firmly on the leg assembly.

Assembling the table involves making up three subassemblies—joining a pair of legs to each side rail and joining the slats to the end rails—then joining the subassemblies. The top is a gravity fit; it's heavy enough to stay put without adhesives or fasteners.

OAK PORCH SWING

Turn-of-the-Century Graciousness for Your Porch

A porch is an architectural reminder to take time out. This porch swing is a further inducement. There is nothing practical whatsoever about a legless bench that hangs from the ceiling. You sit in it because you want to relax, without apologies.

This swing is just a generic, traditional-looking swing, not a replica of any specific swing. Nevertheless, it evokes the turn-of-the-century spirits of family, comfort,

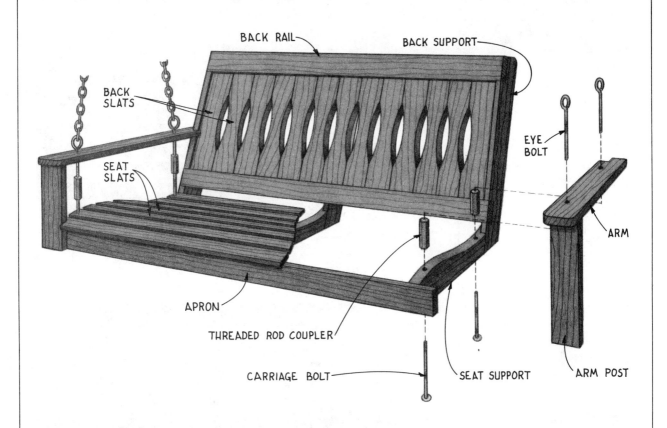

BACK RAIL

BACK SUPPORT

BACK SLATS

SEAT SLATS

EYE BOLT

ARM

APRON

THREADED ROD COUPLER

CARRIAGE BOLT

SEAT SUPPORT

ARM POST

SHOPPING LIST

LUMBER

15 bd. ft. 4/4 white oak
5 bd. ft. 5/4 white oak
4 bd. ft. 8/4 white oak

HARDWARE AND SUPPLIES

1 box #6 × 2" galvanized drywall-type screws
1 box #6 × 1¼" galvanized drywall-type screws
4 pcs. ⁵⁄₁₆" × 6" eyebolts
4 pcs. ⁵⁄₁₆" × 7" carriage bolts

HARDWARE AND SUPPLIES—CONTINUED

4 pcs. ⁵⁄₁₆" threaded rod couplers
4 pcs. ⁵⁄₁₆" nuts
2 pcs. ⅜" × 3" eyescrews
Chain as required
Resorcinol glue

FINISH

Clear water repellent or clear exterior finish

CUTTING LIST

PIECE	NUMBER	THICKNESS	WIDTH	LENGTH	MATERIAL
Back supports	3	¾"	3"	24½"	4/4 oak
Seat supports	3	1½"	3"	21½"	8/4 oak
Back slats	13	⅜"	3½"	15"	5/4 oak
Back rails	2	¾"	3"	47"	4/4 oak
Apron	1	¾"	2⅜"	51"	4/4 oak
Seat slats	7	¾"	2¼"	47"	4/4 oak
Arm posts	2	¾"	3½"	11"	4/4 oak
Arms	2	¾"	3½"	24½"	4/4 oak

TOOL LIST

Backsaw
Band saw
Bar or pipe clamps
Clamps
Drill
   $\frac{5}{16}$" dia. bit
   Countersink bit
   Pilot hole bit
Hammer
Jointer
Paintbrush
Planer
Pliers
Radial arm saw
   Dado set
Router
   ¼" rounding-over bit
   ⅜" rabbeting bit
Saber saw
Sander(s)
Sandpaper
Sawhorses
Screwdriver
Table saw
   Dado cutter
   Miter gauge
Tack cloth
Tape measure
Wrenches

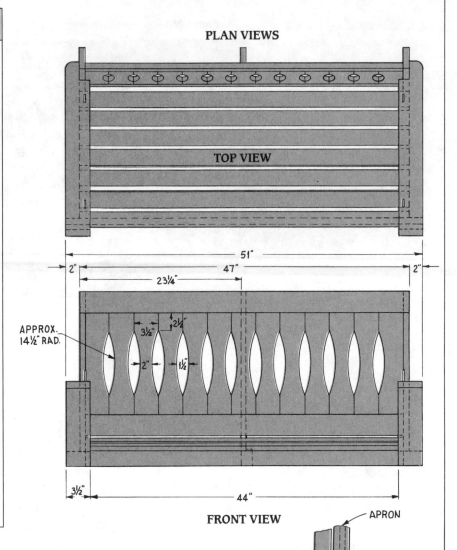

PLAN VIEWS

TOP VIEW

FRONT VIEW

APPROX.
14½" RAD.

SECTION VIEW

APRON

ARM POST

SEAT SUPPORT

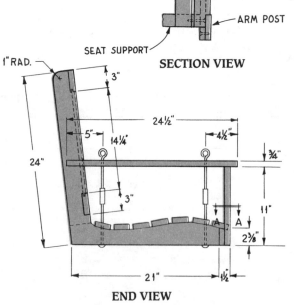

END VIEW

and moderation in life's pace. The swing is quietly reminiscent of Victorian porch swings. Rather than elaborate gingerbread, though, it has a series of ellipses piercing the back. To me, this one belongs on a Victorian house's porch. Or on whatever porch you have.

Builder's Notes

This project offers few perils for most woodworkers. You do have to prepare hardwood stock in three thicknesses. And the joinery—mortise-and-tenon joints, lap joints—*sounds* a bit advanced, perhaps. But you *can* deal with these challenges.

Materials. Oak is a wood that was especially popular around the turn of the century. When you think of Victorian furnishings, you think of oak. As often as not, *dark* oak. So oak is a natural choice for this swing.

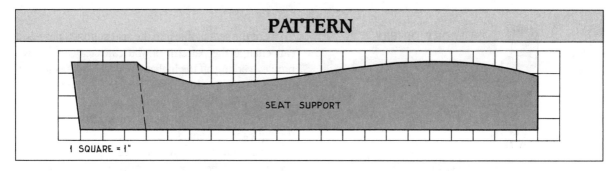

PATTERN

SEAT SUPPORT

1 SQUARE = 1"

A note on *dark* is in order. Turn-of-the-century furnishings were dark because they were stained or fumed to make them that way. We liked the natural blonde of white oak, so we eschewed stains, using a clear finish. As long as the finish is maintained, the blondeness should survive. Unfinished and left in the weather (even if under roof), oak will darken.

Having selected oak, we picked white oak over red oak because it has more decay resistance than the red oak.

Hardwoods usually are stocked in a rough-sawn state. If you don't have a jointer and a planer, you must have the supplier dress the wood. The shopping and cutting lists assume you will resaw the 5/4 (five-quarter) stock to obtain the ⅜-inch stock for the slats.

The swing is assembled largely with screws. The only glued joints are the laps that join the two elements of the supports. The back slats are captured between the rails, which in turn are captured by the supports. And screws affix the rails to the supports. Screws also affix the seat slats, the arm posts, and the arms. In all cases, the screws used are the galvanized drywall type.

The hardware used to hang the swing shouldn't be hard to find at a respectable hardware store. If you shop at a place that displays its hardware in blister packs, there's one item you might not find: the threaded rod coupler. Looking like an overgrown hex nut, it links two threaded rods or bolts. You turn each rod about ½ inch into the coupler.

Tools and techniques. Though the swing looks pretty sophisticated, building it doesn't require sophisticated equipment operated with uncanny proficiency. If you have a shop with the basics—a table saw and assorted portable power tools—you should be okay. A band saw will expedite cutting the back slats and ease cutting the seat supports.

The joinery isn't tough, just a tad tedious. The mortise-and-tenon joints that link the back rails and back slats might easily be called tongue-and-groove joints. The mortise is really an open-ended groove, the tenons are offset, so that forming them is a matter of cutting a rabbet across each end of every slat. The tedium stems from the number of slats to be worked.

The one operation that's unusual among the projects in this book is resawing. The back slats are only ⅜ inch thick. Resawing thicker stock will save an enormous amount of time and wood. Working 4/4 (four-quarter) lumber down to ⅜ inch on a planer takes a long time, and it turns an awful lot of good wood into shavings, too. From a slightly heftier 5/4 board, you can resaw two ⅜-inch boards. Although the band saw generally is regarded as the best tool for resawing, swing-builder Phil Gehret resawed the slats on the table saw.

1**. Make the support frames.** Begin the construction process by building the three support frames. Cut the three back supports from ¾-inch-thick stock, and the three seat supports from 1½-inch-thick stock. Make them a bit long to provide a margin of error at the joints. Lay out the laps, as shown in the *Support Joinery* drawing; as you can see, only the seat supports are lapped. Note that the lap's shoulder is 7½ degrees off square, so the back will lean back. The lap is cut into the outside face of the two outer seat supports, but it can be in either face of the center seat support.

A radial arm saw equipped with a dado cutter may be the best tool for cutting the laps. It allows you to see the lap as you cut, and you can hog out the full ¾-inch depth of the lap in a single pass. (A router also allows you to see the cut as you work, but you should only trim about ³⁄₁₆ inch from the lap with each pass, so the process will take longer.) Remember that the outer supports are mirror images of each other, not duplicates. And if you make the laps a tad longer than specified (because of your margin for error), be sure you leave yourself enough room for the seat.

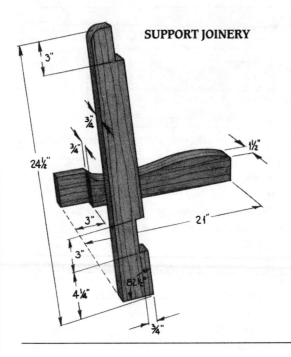

SUPPORT JOINERY

Cut the seat profile into the seat supports next. You can enlarge the pattern, or you can create your own profile, working off the high and low points indicated on the *End View.* In either case, transfer the profile to the three supports, then cut on the band saw.

Notch and trim the back supports next. Round off the top back corners of the three supports on the band saw or with a saber saw. All three must be notched to accommodate the back rails. The two outer supports get 3-inch-wide, ¾-inch-deep notches, as shown in the *End View.* The middle support has to be reduced in width from its top to the lower notch's bottom edge so the back assembly will nestle into it. Lay out these notches and cut them on the band saw.

Finally, glue up the pairs of supports, and secure the joints with clamps until the glue has dried. Trim both ends of each board at the joints, as shown in the *End View.*

2. Cut the back rails. Cut the two back rails to length. Round the top front edge of the upper rail, using a router and a ¼-inch rounding-over bit.

Plow a ¼-inch-wide, ⅜-inch-deep groove in one edge of each, using either a router or a dado blade on a table saw. The back slats' tenons will be held within these grooves. For the best appearance, you can make these stopped grooves, so they won't be exposed on the ends. Or you can glue a scrap of the working stock in the grooves at the ends. We left the grooves open.

Finish up the rails by sanding them smooth.

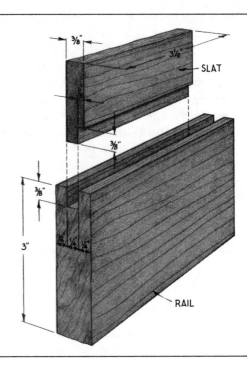

SLAT-TO-RAIL JOINERY

3. Resaw stock for the back slats. The back slats are cut from ⅜-inch-thick stock. Since this is not a standard thickness, you'll either have to pay extra to have the required amount of stock prepared for you, or you'll have to make it yourself. The best way to generate this stock is by resawing 5/4 stock.

The band saw is generally regarded as the best tool for resawing, but unless you have a thickness planer,

you may be better off doing the work on the table saw. The table saw blade makes a pretty wide kerf, but it is rigid and yields a sawed face that's parallel to the face that bore on the rip fence. You can, therefore, clean up the sawed face on the jointer or with a belt sander, and be reasonably assured both faces will be true. The band saw blade, on the other hand, while it does make a narrow kerf, tends to wander even when you use a fence

TIP

While it's possible to resaw stock free-hand on the band saw, you can be more accurate if you guide the board with a pivot. Clamped to the saw table as shown, the pivot braces the workpiece, keeping the cut from wandering, thus helping you to achieve a uniform thickness. The advantage of the pivot over a fence is that you can shift the feed angle without interrupting the cut. Using a marking gauge, or just a pencil and rule, mark a cutting line on the unjointed edge of each piece to be resawed. Cut with the jointed face of the stock held firmly against the pivot, turning the board as necessary—adjusting the feed angle, in other words—to hold to the line.

The pivot is made by cutting a piece of wood or plywood to approximately the shape shown, then cutting bevels on the edge, so the workpiece rides against a point rather than a surface.

(If the blade guide in the photo seems high, it is that way for a reason. The conventional wisdom is that the guide should

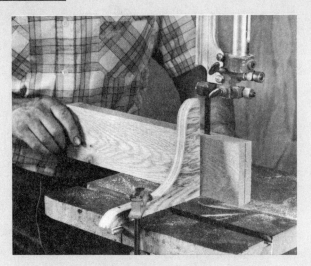

be set as close to the top of the workpiece as possible to minimize blade deflection. The problem is that the blade can deflect inside the cut. If the guide is close to the wood, you can't see the deflection. If it is well above the wood, as shown, you can see the deflection and react by adjusting the angle of feed.)

or pivot, yielding a somewhat uneven sawed face. And this can lead to unevenness and taper in the jointed or sanded piece.

Regardless of the approach you take, prepare the stock by squaring one face and one edge on a jointer; the board must rest squarely on the saw table and against the fence or pivot.

Use a featherboard to control the stock when resawing on the table saw. Position the featherboard just shy of the saw blade (so it doesn't pinch the blade) and tight enough against the stock to prevent kickback—its main purpose. Set the saw to cut just about halfway through the stock. Make one pass, then flip the board end for end and, keeping the same face against the fence as in the previous pass, make a second cut.

4. **Cut and tenon the back slats.** If necessary after resawing, cut the back slats to the size specified by the "Cutting List."

Turn one slat into a pattern for cutting arcs in the rest. First, find and mark reference points on the slat: the ends

of the arc and its high point. The arc begins (or ends) 2½ inches from either end; at its midpoint, its rise is ¾ inch. Connect these marks with a curved line. This line is roughly the arc of a 14½-inch-radius circle. Cut this slat, then use it as a template to lay out others, then

TIP

Laying out the back slats can be done any number of ways. You can use a template. Or mark high and low points, then connect the dots freehand.

We used a flexible strip of Formica scrap to form an arc we liked (and that connected the dots), then we traced the arc. To make this a one-man process, and to "capture" the arc so you can trace it again and again, make a short cut into each end of the scrap. Knot a string and catch it in the cut on one end. Flex the strip, then knot the string a second time, catching it in the kerf at the other end. Makes a little bow, like for archery. Mark the appropriate spots on the workpiece, line up the bow, and trace the arc.

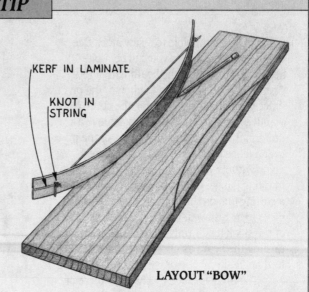

KERF IN LAMINATE

KNOT IN STRING

LAYOUT "BOW"

cut them as well. Note that the two end back slats have only one arc apiece, so hold two slats aside, cutting only a single arc in them. After cutting all the slats, sand them, particularly the sawed edges.

Tenon the slats next. The tenons are offset, so cutting them is a matter of rabbeting each end of every slat. You can do this on a table saw using a standard blade and a tenoning jig. Or you can use a ⅜-inch rabbeting bit in a router to form them. To save setup time, Phil used the table saw's standard blade and made multiple cuts to form the tenons. Set the rip fence ⅜ inch from the *outside* of the blade to control the length of the tenons. Using the miter gauge to guide the slat, make a pass with the slat end butted against the fence, cutting the shoulder. A couple more passes will complete the tenon. Before cutting the slats, test the setup on a scrap, and test the fit of the tenon in the grooves in the rails. Adjust the thickness of the tenons to get a snug fit.

Save layout and cutting time by stacking and cutting three or four slats at a time (obviously, with the pattern marked on the top slat). This is something to do on a band saw, not with a saber saw. Hold the stack together, all the slats in alignment, with tape. That way you can focus entirely on cutting accurately. Any tape will do—masking tape, duct tape, even packing tape.

5. **Assemble the back.** You usually begin an assembly this big with a dry run. Partly to test how the joints fit, but also to practice the routine so you don't dribble glue all over while you try to figure how to fit two parts together, and so the glue doesn't set up before you're ready. You can cut to the chase here, because you really don't *need* glue. The slats won't fall out, since they're captured by the rails and the outer supports. And the rails are attached to the supports with screws. No

glue is needed there, either.

Fitting the rail-and-slat subassembly into the notches in the three back supports will doubtlessly go best if you have help. If you have to go it alone, keep the rail-and-slat assembly together with two or three bar or pipe clamps. The assembly fits into the notches cut into the back supports. With the assembly in place, drill two pilot holes through it at each place a frame member rests against a back support. Drive 2-inch screws into the holes.

6. **Cut and attach the apron and seat slats.**
Cut the apron to size, beveling the top edge at 75 degrees to meet the front seat slat. Sand the apron. Then, holding the apron in place, drill two pilot holes through it and into each seat frame. Drive 2-inch screws into the holes.

Cut the seat slats from ¾-inch stock, and round what will be the exposed edges with a router and a ¼-inch rounding-over bit. Lay out the slats on the seat supports, arranging them an equal distance apart. With a pilot hole bit, drill two countersunk pilot holes through each slat into each support. Drive a 2-inch galvanized screw into each hole.

Finally, drill holes for the suspension hardware. As you will note on the *End View,* the holes penetrate the second slat (from the front) and the last (or rearmost) slat. Back out two screws on each side: the front screw in the second slat, the rear screw in the last slat. Drill ⁵⁄₁₆-inch-diameter holes at these four points, through both the seat slats and the supports below.

---

7. **Cut and attach the posts and arms.** Cut the arm posts and arms to size. Fit the posts to the swing assembly, marking the front seat slat for the notches that are necessary to accommodate the posts. (See the *Section View.*) Cut the notches with a backsaw. This *can* be done with the slat in place—the post will conceal any scuffing of the apron that results—but you can easily back out the screws and remove the slat to notch it. Before machining the post edges with a router and a ¼-inch rounding-over bit, stand each post in place, noting the edges that will be exposed and marking where the rounded edges should blend into the rounded edges of adjoining parts. Rout the posts.

To install the posts, drive two 1¼-inch screws through the apron and into the post back, and drive a

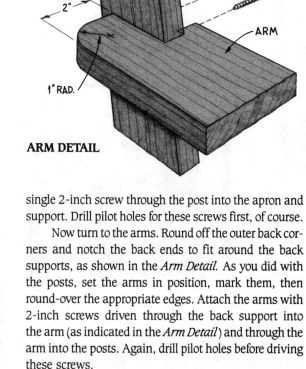

ARM DETAIL

single 2-inch screw through the post into the apron and support. Drill pilot holes for these screws first, of course.

Now turn to the arms. Round off the outer back corners and notch the back ends to fit around the back supports, as shown in the *Arm Detail.* As you did with the posts, set the arms in position, mark them, then round-over the appropriate edges. Attach the arms with 2-inch screws driven through the back support into the arm (as indicated in the *Arm Detail*) and through the arm into the posts. Again, drill pilot holes before driving these screws.

Finally, drill holes on the arms for the suspension hardware. These holes must align with those drilled earlier through the seat slats and seat supports.

The arm posts nestle against the apron and the front seat slat. Secure each one by running in two 1¼-inch screws from the back of the apron, as shown, and a 2-inch screw through the front of the post and the apron into the seat support.

The holes in the arms for the suspension hardware must be directly above the holes already bored in the slats and supports. *Left:* To "capture" the location of a hole in the seat, place a combination square on an arm, as shown, and align its rule with the hole below. Mark the edge of the arm. *Right:* Reposition the square to extend this mark across the top of the arm. Find a point along this line, ¾ inch in from the inside edge of the arm, and drill a 5⁄16-inch-diameter hole for the eyebolt.

8. **Finish the swing.** Sand any areas of the swing that need a touch-up. Apply whatever finish you've

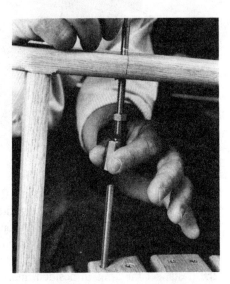

chosen. Because we wanted to show off the natural beauty of the oak used to make the swing, Phil applied two coats of Deft, a clear finish, to the swing shown.

Now install the suspension hardware. Insert the carriage bolts up through the holes in the supports and seat their heads with a tap or two of a hammer. Drop the eyebolts through the holes in the arms. Turn a nut onto one bolt in each pair, then link the pair with a threaded coupling. Hand-tighten the nut against the coupler, then use a pair of wrenches to further tighten the parts.

The eyebolts and carriage bolts come together like this. Turn a regular machine nut onto either the eyebolt (as here) or the carriage bolt. Follow it with a threaded coupler, turning the coupler until the bolt is about halfway through. Hand-tighten the nut against the coupler, then jam them together by tightening them with wrenches. Now thread the coupler onto the other bolt, turning the bolt-nut-coupler assembly until the other bolt is as far into the coupler as it will go.

9. **Hang the swing.** Suspend the swing from framework of substance, like the joists bearing the porch ceiling or the porch-roof rafters—it's got to support the dynamic weight of two or more "swingers," after all. Eyeball the likely trajectory of the swing, and try to minimize the chance that it will hit walls or railings. Pick a pair of joists or rafters that are at least as far apart as the width of the swing. Make sure the two points are on the same level. (Although you can hang it from points at two different heights, it won't swing evenly.) Drill pilot holes and turn eyescrews into them.

Attach the chain to the swing's eyebolts by opening the eyes enough to slip links over them. Close the eyes. Run chain from the eyebolts to the eyescrews, and open the eyes of the screws to hold the links that will put the swing at the right height. Close the eyes, and remove the excess links unless you anticipate adjusting the swing's height.

From time to time, check that the eyescrews are still securely anchored in the joists or rafters. And bring a couple of wrenches out to make sure that the lock nuts and threaded couplers are snug against each other.